NARRATIVE AND THE NATURAL LAW

NARRATIVE
AND THE NATURAL LAW

An Interpretation of Thomistic Ethics

Pamela M. Hall

University of Notre Dame Press
Notre Dame

Manufactured in the United States of America

Paperback printed in 1998
Reprinted in 2008

Library of Congress Cataloging-in-Publication Data

Hall, Pamela M.
    Narrative and the natural law : an interpretation of
    Thomistic Ethics / by Pamela M. Hall.
       p.   cm.
    Includes bibliographical references and index.
    ISBN 10: 0-268-01477-9 (cloth : alk. paper)
    ISBN 13: 978-0-268-01485-8 (pbk : alk. paper)
    ISBN 10: 0-268-01485-X (pbk : alk. paper)
     1. Natural law. 2. Thomas, Aquinas, Saint, 1225?-1274.
    Summa theologica.   I. Title.
    K447.T452H35   1994
    340'.112—dc20   94-15465
                                          CIP

∞ *This book is printed on acid-free paper.*

CONTENTS

ACKNOWLEDGMENTS

This study has its intellectual roots in work I did with Alasdair MacIntyre as a graduate student at Vanderbilt University. As my teacher and dissertation advisor, Professor MacIntyre instructed me with his characteristic thoroughness, fairness, and insight; my thanks to him. Likewise, Mark D. Jordan, of the University of Notre Dame, has provided unstinting encouragement and guidance to me, on this project and more generally.

Many colleagues and friends at Emory and in Atlanta have given me invaluable support in the writing of this book. I owe my colleague in Philosophy at Emory, Thomas R. Flynn, a special debt of thanks in this regard. Also at Emory, Wendy Farley in the Religion Department and Martine Watson Brownley in the Institute for Women's Studies have been wise and steadfast friends and colleagues; their friendships have enriched me. Likewise, Juliet Rumble, Susan Fraysse, and Mary Threlkeld have been considerate and sustaining friends in my years in Atlanta.

I thank the University Research Council at Emory University for granting me release time from teaching for early research on this book. I am also grateful to Jeannette Morgenroth, my editor at the University of Notre Dame Press, for her good counsel and her enthusiasm for my project.

Earlier versions of sections from chapters one, two, and five have been published previously in *Political Theory* within my article "Goerner on Thomistic Natural Law," vol. 18, no. 4 (November 1990), 638–655, © 1990 by Sage Publications, Inc. Reprinted by permission of Sage Publications, Inc. Some portions of chapters two and five were published in *Medieval Philosophy and Theology* as "Towards a Narrative Understanding of Thomistic Natural Law," vol. 2 (1992), 53–73.

NL

- intends NL to serve as standard
  for justice accessible to all
  rational cultures

  ↳ so guides human action

↳ to explain is to
   ~~determine~~ determine
   how is NL promulgated?

   ↳ sight by looking at
      different identified by other trait

- Depdis
- reutsch
  ↳ T ethis
- autonomy
  ↳ dictats
    ↳ speck or
    + moral
    teaching
  ..not sth
  commonsth
  natural law
  + virtue

1. QUESTIONS AND CONCERNS

This book arises in part out of a deep discontent with much recent scholarship on Thomistic ethics. On one side, the *Summa theologiae's* Treatise on Law is often studied, or at least interpreted, autonomously, i.e., without sufficient reference to the rest of the *Summa*. This has certain distorting effects on the construal of Thomistic moral teaching, and I will explain the nature of those distortions in this and following chapters. On the other hand, Thomas's doctrines of grace and the supernatural virtues have been discussed, but typically in unreal isolation from his so-called natural moral philosophy. The account I will put forward in this book attempts to show the connections between the natural law and the virtues, natural and supernatural (or, to use Thomas's terms, acquired and infused). This will entail a discussion of the natural law's relation to the divine law, both Old and New. In particular, I want to describe the ways in which the natural law and prudence work together in Aquinas. Necessarily, this account must merge with another that explains the crucial place of charity in his teleological ethics.

But my project cannot be adequately described as an attempt to secure a faithful exegesis of Thomas's moral teaching; at the same time, I wish to indicate what kinds of issues should be considered by anyone attempting to resolve the problems about the nature of standards of law in relation to prudence in ethics. Some discussion of practical reasoning is entailed here, as well as examination of how practical reasoning is structured by historical contingencies. We are led in turn to the issue of tragic conflict. Elucidating what Thomas has to say on these issues is a

1

demanding task, but necessary, I believe, for a right understanding of his ethics and its full philosophical import.

Thomas intends the natural law to serve as a nonconventional standard of justice accessible to all rational creatures. He describes it as the peculiar way in which rational creatures participate in eternal law.[1] If the natural law is indeed an efficacious guide for human action, it must somehow meet the criteria for all law: as Thomas notes, law must be an ordinance of reason for the common good, made by the appropriate legislator, which must be properly promulgated.[2] Using this basic definition, perhaps the easiest route into my set of concerns is a very simple question: How is the natural law promulgated?

It is my argument in this book that an adequate answer to this question entails an account of the natural law that does full justice to its historical development. This ongoing process presupposes the activity of prudence operating on both the individual and the political levels; the work of prudence is, I argue, in part the very development of the rules of the natural law. But my emphasis on prudence will not neglect the various and complex ways that Thomas sees law as shaping human society and human judgment. I will also address the natural law's relation to other kinds of law.

Let me begin by sketching some of the difficulties which other readers of Aquinas have had with his doctrine of natural law; they raise questions which my own account of Aquinas must answer. I will be engaging as interlocutors those who share a similar purpose in reading Thomas. I will begin with a discussion of two philosophers who, although hardly Thomists, have stated with power some of the central philosophical problems to be encountered by any exegete of Thomistic natural law.[3]

Strauss and Jaffa:
How Natural Is the Natural Law?

Both Leo Strauss and Harry Jaffa have found fault with the standard of exceptionless rules which they take Thomistic natural law to embody. Strauss, in *Natural Right and History*, compares

Aquinas's ethics unfavorably to Aristotle's. Thomas's standard of invariant law lacks the flexibility and the adaptiveness of Aristotelian natural right; likewise, it is unclear in what way the "natural law, as Thomas Aquinas understands it, is natural law strictly speaking, i.e., a law knowable to the unassisted human mind, to the human mind which is not illumined by divine revelation."[4] Strauss recognizes that divine law completes the natural law according to Aquinas; this fact alone renders questionable the efficacy of the natural law as standard.

At any rate, the ultimate consequence of the Thomistic view of natural law is that natural law is practically inseparable not only from natural theology—i.e., from a natural theology which is, in fact, based on belief in biblical revelation—but even from revealed theology.[5]

Strauss interprets modern natural law theorists to be opponents of this Thomistic account, both in terms of the Thomistic submission of reason to revelation and in terms of its standard of inflexible, and (on his view) politically unreasonable, law.

I take both problems—the status of law as adequate ethical standard and the natural law's accessibility to reason—to be crucial in an explanation of Thomistic natural law. Strauss's sketch of Aquinas's natural law theory has the merit of singling out exactly those core issues which Aquinas must answer for the natural law to serve *as* natural law and as a responsible moral standard. First, to the latter issue: Strauss indicates the possible tension, even conflict, between an ethical standard of law and that which allows for the primacy of judgment. This tension will be argued for with even greater emphasis by Martha Nussbaum, to be discussed later. Strauss also invokes the concern of how naturally accessible this standard of natural law is. As we will see in later chapters, this becomes a crucial problem for Thomas in his elaboration of the relation between the Old Law and the *lex naturae*. I will try to show in what ways Strauss's truncated account of Thomas fails to note the relation between his doctrine of natural law and the virtues. My explanation will also clarify the character of the natural law's promulgation to humankind, a topic which is directly related to Strauss's concern with the natural law's accessibility to reason.

Harry Jaffa, in his book *Thomism and Aristotelianism*, which examines Thomas's commentary on the *Nicomachean Ethics* in the light of Thomas's relation to Aristotle, takes up the issue of promulgation raised by Strauss. Jaffa questions whether one condition for all law, according to Aquinas—that it be ordained by the proper legislator—could hold for the natural law.[6] Recognition of the natural law for what it is would imply, on Jaffa'a view, recognition of divine providence: for the natural law to be promulgated adequately to men and women, they must recognize the law as deriving from God as governor of the cosmos. This, Jaffa maintains, cannot be known with certainty apart from divine revelation.

Likewise, Jaffa finds fault with the standard of natural law, constituted by exceptionless rules, in comparison with Aristotelian *phronesis* in its capacity to find the "naturally right" (*ius naturale*). This latter standard of practical wisdom allows for greater flexibility and greater responsibility to the particular circumstance (and here he echoes Strauss). Natural law, on the other hand, commands what is invariably the best; this is certainly important, but the human legislator must also be allowed a certain freedom of play in his or her deliberations about how to achieve the good. The best is not always attainable here and now. As Jaffa says,

> What is naturally best is distinct from what is naturally right. The former is the standard to which the wise legislator looks, in order to know the true *direction* of all sound policy. What is just is what is fitting here and now.[7]

Thus the natural law, insofar as it will not admit of exceptions or revisions, would on Jaffa's view be irresponsibly high minded, refusing to settle for what is attainable here and now.

It will be part of my argument that in fact the version of natural law which is held by Strauss and Jaffa (but by others as well) is elliptical and in some respects inaccurate. Aquinas says a great deal more about what the law is and how it operates than their account suggests. By stressing the ongoing development of the natural law, as well as the need for prudence for this development, I will offer an explanation that (1) describes in what sense the natural law can be considered natural and accessible to reason and (2) describes the ultimate compatibility of the standards of the natural law and prudence. Such an account is crucial in any philosophic defense of Aquinas because the compatibility of natural law and *prudence* (a term I will use as synonymous with *practical wisdom*) bears not only on the issue of whether Thomas or Aristotle be the wiser teacher of ethics, which is the central concern of Strauss and Jaffa. The case against Aquinas may, in fact, be even more damning in this regard than they apparently realized: the standard of prudence is internal to Thomas's own ethics; if the standards of natural law and prudence are incompatible, then Thomistic ethics suffers from internal contradiction.

Let me now continue this discussion of how the natural law has been understood with reference to prudence by looking at two more contemporary philosophers: Martha Nussbaum and E. A. Goerner. Both argue, in very different ways, for the superiority of practical wisdom to the natural law. I will spend comparatively more time with Nussbaum and Goerner in part because they argue their case at greater length and with reference to important connected issues. I take these related concerns to be particularly significant to my own project.

Nussbaum:
Practical Wisdom, Rules,
and Tragic Conflict

One of the most sweeping contemporary critiques of rule following comes from Martha Nussbaum, who in her writings on Greek ethics has constructed a strong argument against any "compatibilist" approach to the relation between practical wisdom and adherence to absolute rules. On her view, practical wisdom and any set of rule-governed precepts and prohibitions constitute alternative, as well as rival, standards of right action. Rule following provides inferior and inadequate ethical guidance, even sometimes producing results that are not only different from practical wisdom, i.e., not optimal, but also positively harmful. Nussbaum seems to suggest that by an unyielding and unrealistic adherence to rules, rule followers, by their inattention to the existing particulars of a situation, may produce events or relations that issue in injury to themselves and others. Nussbaum herself makes explicit reference to Aquinas in only one of the essays I will discuss, but her case against rule following more generally can certainly be applied to Aquinas, as she construes him. I will, in my own exegesis of her position, attempt to construct the strongest argument she might make against him.

In her early commentary on Aristotle's *De motu animalium*, Nussbaum most clearly lays out her case against a system of rule following that she labels *deductivism*. In an interpretive essay accompanying her translation of *De motu animalium*, "Practical Syllogisms and Practical Science," Nussbaum criticizes deductivism as a deeply flawed project in practical reasoning.[8] She assigns deductivism three main tenets which she asserts have been wrongly attributed to Aristotle but may well pertain to Aquinas's Aristotelianism.[9] The first doctrine of such systems is that their "practical principles form a closed, consistent deductive system, beginning with a priori first principles concerning the essence or nature of man."[10] Such principles are taken to be "objectively valid," requiring neither the desires nor the judgments of persons to ratify them. Given this view of rules, all that is necessary for right action is for the agent "to subsume the situation under the relevant rule, plug it into the right place in the hierarchy."[11] Thus the agent has the responsibility to make his or her practical reasoning as correct and scientific as possible by the use of this system; the agent's further responsibility is to bring his or her own desires into harmony with what those rules enjoin. Secondly, in justifying his or her actions, the agent must necessarily be able to cite the rule appropriate to the case. In such justification, there can be only one suitable rule; no alternative, competing candidates are to be found. Within the deductivist's system, no "incommensurable claims" exist,[12] so there can be no conflict or competition between distinct obligations. Further, the examination of any situation must always yield one best rule or response, so that alternative rules are always inferior to some degree and thereby not equal competitors. Lastly, in a statement of the third tenet of deductivism, Nussbaum explains that the theory often describes reasonable and moral action as independent of desires: reason is taken to motivate by itself. This claim she puts aside, however, as peripheral to the character of deductivism in order to direct attention to its first two tenets.

What lies behind the deductivist drive, behind these chief characteristics, is something else again; Nussbaum speaks of the motives for the composition of such neat, consistent systems in two ways. First, in her *De motu animalium* essays and in "The Discernment of Perception,"[13] she describes the deductivist's "dissatisfaction with the messiness of ordinary attempts at practical reasoning and the hope for a more scientific enterprise that would bring order, even salvation, to troubled men."[14] Nussbaum here assumes that ordinary practical reasoning's "messiness" is due neither to enthymemes, nor to the density of practical concerns, nor to defects in reasoning: rather, it is part of the very character of practical reasoning as such.[15] Deductivists wish neither to acknowledge nor to grapple with the messiness.

In "Practical Syllogisms" and further in *The Fragility of Goodness*, Nussbaum describes the Socrates of the middle dialogues as engaging in just this sort of project. Socrates she represents as engaged in a kind of practical reasoning that strives to measure all goods according to a single scale of value, making calculation tidy and rigorous—but at the expense of the goods' true natures. She here assumes that while judging according to a homogeneous qualitative scale of value may make deliberation neater, the very homogeneity of the scale betrays the real objects and persons it evaluates, which she takes to be heterogeneous in their values and diverse, even elusive, in their natures.[16] Further, this new Socratic *techne* of practical reason will strive to rank most highly those goods less vulnerable to chance, to *tuche*.[17] These less "fragile" goods, when considered constitutive of the best life, will foster what Nussbaum takes to be the aim of this Socratic ethic—self-sufficiency.

On her view, the project of scientific deliberation, having as its goal self-sufficiency, must reject the possibility of tragic conflict; any recognition of tragedy would acknowledge that in certain situations, no choice is good or desirable, and choice itself becomes then an occasion for remorse, even for horror. Instances of such practical conflict can be found in tragedy as well as history: Nussbaum cites such examples as Agamemnon and the soldier, described by Tacitus, charged with the slaying of his own brother, who fought on the opposing side of a civil war. The deductivist strives to construct a system in which such conflict cannot arise and in which tragic emotions (anxiety, horror) are thus warded off. A "coherent set of rules governing every possible situation" would eliminate tragic conflict, eliminate the inescapable remorse accompanying tragic choices, eliminate the confusion, even the precariousness, of a less rigorous model of practical reasoning. On the deductivist's view, once you have the right rule, all is well; indeed, all must be well.

The character of the motive Nussbaum attributes to deductivism is not lofty; one might describe it as an anxious desire to avoid pain and perplexity. But Nussbaum pushes her diagnosis of those dedicated to such scientific practical reasoning even further. In her essay on Henry James's *The Golden Bowl*, she examines one example of such a moral agent in the person of Maggie Verver.[18] Loving her widowed father intensely, desiring to maintain the close bond they have had, Maggie unknowingly slights her new husband by not forming a close tie with him. In her desire to be the perfect daughter, she is thereby an imperfect wife; further, in the early days of their marriage, she is wholly unconscious of her failing.

Maggie's desire not to hurt her father and her early ignorance of the hurt she does her spouse Amerigo are connected for Nussbaum with a broader ethical concern—to remain guiltless in all things, never to do anyone harm: "She wants, this woman, to have a flawless life."[19] Exactly this anxious (and hubristic?) desire produces both Maggie's neglect of Amerigo and her ignorance of it. Nussbaum links Maggie's simplistic, "girlish" notion of right action with a failure to see what actually is and a failure to see what is needed to remedy the harm her blindness has produced. Later, in describing the superior qualities of practical wisdom, this breakdown in the perception of rule followers will prove important. Nussbaum characterizes Maggie's failure as

> an inability in any area of her life to see values, including persons, emerge as distinct ends in their own right. In every case they are rounded, accommodated, not recognized, insofar as their claims collide with other claims.[20]

What Nussbaum seems to quarrel with here is not just the notion of a rule-governed morality but the notion of there being a set of descriptions of types of action adequate for moral direction. Her position commits her to the view that no set of rules, however detailed, could be framed antecedently to take account of particular situations sufficiently; moreover, no set of descriptions can be known in advance that would specify all the morally relevant features of a situation. No set of rules, no single scale of value, can do justice to the heterogeneity of the world. These are Nussbaum's a prioris. This ability to see the value of each thing in itself, and not through the filter of a consistent, closed system or according to a single scale of evaluation, is what constitutes genuine moral objectivity, and part of what constitutes practical wisdom. Seeing things as they are entails, Nussbaum presupposes, seeing the conflicting claims they make upon one. For her, incommensurable claims are the stock experience of the virtuous person.

> The world of *The Golden Bowl* is a fallen world—a world, that is, in which innocence cannot be and is not safely preserved, a world where values and loves are so pervasively in tension one with another that there is no safe human experience of a perfect fidelity to all throughout life. . . . There are better and worse choices, naturally, within this tangled world; but it is childlike to refuse to see that it *is* in this way tangled, for this is a feature of our situation as creatures operating in a world of nature.[21]

For this reason she takes Socratic practical science to be so misguided: it gives the lie to accurate experience of the world.

It falsifies the world in order to insulate the agent from painful realities. It is likewise part of the deductivist motive, a motive in which Thomas may share.[22]

But Nussbaum does permit to rules a more limited role in ethics. In her article, "The Discernment of Perception," she allows for the application of rules within certain constraints.[23] So long as they retain revisability and are not given pride of place in deliberation, rules can be useful. They can be, first of all, aids in moral education, being "summaries" of past judgments by the practically wise.[24] Also, rules can serve as guides or checks in the event of the need for rapid decisions or when passion or personal interest leads an agent to mistrust his or her own judgment. Further, they can instruct even mature moral agents in their confrontation with new situations, "guiding them tentatively in their approach to the particular, helping them pick out its salient features."[25] Nussbaum extends this point:

> Perception, we might say, is a process of loving conversation between rules and concrete responses, general conceptions and unique cases, in which the general articulates the particular and is in turn further articulated by it. . . . The general is dark, incommunicative, if it is not realized in a concrete image; but a concrete image or description would be inarticulate, indeed mad, if it contained no universals. . . . In the end, the general is only as good as its role in the correct articulation of the concrete.[26]

Clearly, rules of the sort that Nussbaum favors could not be exceptionless in character, prohibiting or prescribing always. Instead, her rules would have a different content, prohibiting or prescribing generally or for the most part. Further, the descriptions of actions within such rules would only be initial approximations, open to, even requiring, revision. As such, it would be misleading to say that these rules admit of exceptions at all since they are at best general counsels or directives to be applied, refined, or even ignored given particular circumstances. Only more absolute prohibitions and prescriptions, with more precise formulation, can accurately be said to admit of exceptions.

The most significant features of Nussbaum's argument for the superiority of practical wisdom over deductivism will provide a focus in my own account of Thomistic natural law. To begin with, I must explain the character of the rules of the natural law and the mechanism of their application. I take it that Nussbaum fails to recognize what is required in successful rule following: an understanding of how to apply the rule in the light of its purpose. Is it ever possible, in a situation of uncertainty, merely to "plug in" a rule in order to discover what to do? Someone must select the rule; someone must decide how to use it. Thus Nussbaum will enable us to explore further and more deeply what is really at issue in the supposed tension (alleged by Strauss and Jaffa as well) between an ethics of law and an ethics of virtue. I will argue that Thomas's characterization of our discovery of the natural law, as an activity of practical reasoning, precisely requires the virtues which Nussbaum denies rule followers.

What is further at issue, for Nussbaum, is acknowledgment of tragedy. She ties deductivist rule following to moral blindness and to the refusal to acknowledge the heterogeneity of goods in the world. *Tragic* is called our inability to satisfy fully all our ethical demands in this "fallen" world; tragic, too, may be the deductivist denial that the world is thus heterogeneous. In the first, the fault may be in the world; in the latter, in ourselves. I believe that Nussbaum is right to see important consequences for ethics in the matter of tragedy and in the preference of rules to virtues as an ethical standard. I wish to explore Thomas's own position on the issue of tragedy. Whether Thomas falls under her criticisms of deductivists remains to be decided. But Thomas's acknowledgment of the historical nature of our ethical knowledge, as I will describe it, bears upon the possibility for tragic conflict or loss in important ways.

Next I will turn to a philosopher who, drawing on Aquinas himself, constructs an account of the natural law's promulgation that requires the primacy of prudence to the natural law. He takes up the same issues as Strauss, Jaffa, and Nussbaum, but advances a position different from theirs in important ways. I will suggest, first here and at greater length later, why his account cannot succeed.

Goerner:
Learning the Natural Law

E. A. Goerner has cleared important ground in the philosophical study of Aquinas. In two articles on Thomistic ethics, he rejects Aquinas's traditional classification as a natural law theorist.[27] Goerner identifies the presence of two ethical standards in Aquinas's thought, natural law and natural right; here he advances Strauss's and Nussbaum's concerns while proving a more adequate exegete of Aquinas. Goerner takes natural law to be a set of exceptionless rules prescribing or constraining action. In contrast the natural right theorist, of which Aristotle is an example, holds that rules "are, at best, generalizations that are not universally valid but are changeable according to circumstances."[28] The real criterion of natural right ultimately must be the judgment of the virtuous person.

Goerner provides an account of how these two very different standards function within Thomistic ethics. He takes up Aquinas's own distinction between intrinsic and extrinsic principles of actions.[29] The intrinsic principles, moving the moral agent by love of the good, include the virtues. The extrinsic principles of action are law and grace, both of which in some sense move from without. Law is, minimally, constraint upon the vicious, imposing penalty for violations; optimally, it is "a propaedeutic to virtue."[30] Nonetheless, law has not the perfection of fully virtuous action, and Thomas's ethics is incompletely understood without attention to his teaching on the virtues: "a full understanding of Thomas's natural ethics must rest on his teaching about natural virtue rather than about natural law."[31]

In showing how virtue is a superior standard to law, Goerner rejects the conventional explanation that the difference between the law-abiding bad person and the truly good person is of motive only. On this view, the vicious person would obey out of fear;

the virtuous, from understanding and desire of the good. If this were accurate, then law would still be the ultimate standard in Thomistic ethics, since the content of the law would still be understood to embody fully "the content of morality."[32] And to contest this "conventional view" of Thomistic ethics,[33] Goerner turns to a more detailed discussion of how natural law operates as a *disciplina* for virtue that secures God's purposes without violating human freedom.

Building on an example drawn from Aquinas himself, Goerner explains how the natural law both educates and censures. In discussing how it is that certain people seem ignorant of the natural law,[34] Aquinas cites the instance of the "German robbers," who sustained themselves for generations by the practice of raiding other communities (as spoken of by Julius Caesar in *De bello gallico*). Goerner explains that the Germans in fact learned the natural law, slowly and painfully, from the consequences of breaking it.[35] Their long-term robbery led to the depletion of their neighbors' resources and consequently to their own poverty. The Germans were then forced to set up a more stable way of life and to abandon the custom of raiding. Goerner wishes to term the robbers' experience of the consequences of robbery, and their subsequent changes, an education by natural law. But this rational discovery of consequences and the bowing to the inevitable that is the motive of such social reform require, according to Goerner, no real virtue. Law precisely compels out of fear. For this reason, he calls natural law "the bad man's view of natural right."[36]

In a later article, Goerner specifies in what ways the standard of natural right, constituted by the judgment of the "good man," is superior to natural law.[37] He has already rejected the view that the two standards are really identical in content. Through a subtle reading of Aquinas's discussion of equity and its relation to legal justice,[38] Goerner argues that Aquinas takes equity to "transcend" legal justice. The intention of the lawgiver, as grasped by the prudent man or woman in exercising equity, takes final precedence over any actual code of laws. The intention cannot be stated in any universally applicable set of verbal rules or laws because human acts "vary in an infinity of ways." . . . Consequently, no formulation of natural law, but the singular intentions of one whose soul is an analogue of the providential justice of the God of nature, is the perfect standard of naturally right action.[39]

Thus on Goerner's view natural law and practical wisdom are at best functionally compatible. The law enforces a minimal obedience from the vicious; when real virtue is achieved, the law becomes obsolete or unnecessary—it is "transcended." Indeed the prudence of the just person functions in the creation and application of any code of laws. Goerner interprets Aquinas as asserting that law and virtue are supplementary standards; each constitutes the morality of an individual at a certain stage of the moral life. But the judgment of the virtuous person emerges as the superior standard in the superior stage.

What Goerner has overlooked, however, is what it means for a person or people to possess knowledge of the natural law *qua* natural law. Natural law, according to Aquinas, is not just a means for holding together the social order; nor is it a means for achieving technological advancement, as Goerner seems to say in his discussion of the German robbers.[40] The natural law is for educating people into the life of virtue. How this education is accomplished is the question at the core of my dispute with Goerner.

Goerner argues that the Germans, by breaking the precept of the natural law against robbery, "suffered" the consequences of living in a society that preyed upon other communities' resources. Part of the consequences, Goerner narrates, included the eventual collapse of the Roman economy, unable to support such large-scale raiding.[41] This collapse helped to teach the Germans "the relationship between behavior outside the rule and the natural consequences of that behavior. Then the consequences are seen as punishments for violating the order of nature."[42] The collapse also prompted the marauding German communities to order themselves in a more stable way, with laws respecting ownership of property. This reorganization leads Goerner to claim, "They had learned from nature itself the precept forbidding raiding."[43]

But what have the robbers learned? And who did the learning? To begin with the latter question: All those generations of Germans who lived from the time of Julius Caesar, upon whose testimony Aquinas and Goerner both rely, up to the decade before the collapse of the Roman Empire apparently learned no lesson at all, except perhaps that crime pays.[44] Thus not all bad men learn from their breaches of the natural law, but only some of them. And what has this minority learned? According to Goerner, the Germans learned the badness of robbery by looking at its natural consequences. What is not explained is in what ways these consequences are seen to illumine the virtue or vice of the actions that produced them. Goerner fails to explain what makes possible the Germans' evaluation of their robbery as bad.

For the Germans to identify certain undesirable consequences as penalties would require knowledge of a standard of justice which Goerner seems to deny them (lacking as they are in prudence). Thus he may separate prudence and the natural law too completely for the natural law to serve the educative function he imputes to it. In fact, Goerner provides no systematic account of the relationship of natural law to prudence and of the part played by this relationship in moral education. As a story in moral development, he leaves obscure how the Germans move from baseness to virtue.

This educative function of natural law I wish to take most seriously. I said at the beginning of this chapter that many reservations and criticisms regarding Thomistic natural law can be summarized in the question, How is the natural law promulgated? I will answer this by explaining that it is learned; the promulgation of the *lex naturae* is accomplished as it is learned by individuals and communities. Acquisition of the natural law is inseparable from the law's pedagogical function; we are instructed by the natural law in the discovery of it.

Let me take note of one related feature of Goerner's exegesis. His description of the "re-education" of the Germans has the merit of attempting to represent, in lived terms, what learning the natural law is like. His account suggests that the acquisition of the natural law is a process that may go on over a period of time; it also suggests that the customs and beliefs of an entire community are very much bound up with what is recognized to be natural law. I will extend this emphasis upon the social and historical dimensions of the natural law. In this respect, I believe Goerner is closer to the truth of Thomas's view of natural law than many other interpreters of Aquinas. This brings me to a brief discussion of some contemporary Thomists and their interpretation of the natural law.

Finnis and Grisez:
Natural Law without Nature

Up to this point, I have omitted from the discussion the natural law theorists perhaps most to be noted, John Finnis and Germain Grisez. Their work, within and outside Catholic moral philosophy, has served to revive general interest in the standard of the natural law. Their joint view of natural law, which began with controversial rereadings of Thomas, has since been offered as a theory in its own right that is distinct from Aquinas and other natural law theorists.[45] Beginning with the laudable aims of eschewing the legalism of other interpretations of natural law, and wishing to take seriously the practical nature of practical reason, Finnis and Grisez offer a theory which, on their own view, is both nonteleological and nondeontological.[46] Their renunciation of teleology arises from, among other reasons, their denial of a determinate *telos* to human life. Finnis and Grisez repeatedly endorse the Humean separation of ought and is, a dictum that they take teleological claims to violate. As they say, "from a set of theoretical premises, one cannot logically derive any practical truth, since sound reasoning does not introduce what is not in the premises."[47] Against deontological ethics, they contend it is essential to take account of human desires in characterizing human fulfillment.

According to Finnis and Grisez, the first principle of practical reason (a term employed by Aquinas),[48] "Good is to be done and pursued, and evil is to be avoided," is not itself a moral precept. It is premoral, specifying formally the character of practical reason. In this point at least they claim the company of Aquinas. The first principle establishes constraints for moral action by "prohibiting pointlessness," at least insofar as it requires that pointlessness be "eliminated" when it is discovered in action.[49] Apparently, the premoral precept, when in play, works to direct human choices towards the goal of human fulfillment.

What is the goal of human fulfillment? Practical reason aims at realizing the enjoyment of basic human goods to which we have access by virtue of our natural inclination to them. The actual list of basic goods differs slightly as Finnis and Grisez develop their theory, but one later catalogue includes life, knowledge and the appreciation of beauty, excellence in work and play, harmony with others, harmony of self, a harmony of choices with one's judgments, and religion in some form.[50]

Finnis and Grisez characterize our knowledge of these goods as "self-evident," insofar as we recognize that they are desirable for their own sake when we experience them. Thus they do not claim a priori knowledge of the basic goods. They emphatically deny that one in any way deduces these goods from the first principle of practical reason. Likewise, they hold that these goods are not derived from any metaphysical or anthropological theory of human nature. A priori knowledge, deduction from first principles, or derivation of goods from metaphysical or anthropological claims would depart from the nonteleological, nondeontological frame. Human fulfillment can be specified in no simple or determinate way; rather, one may organize and implement the enjoyment of basic goods in a variety of ways within the constraints of "harmonies" of different kinds which figure as basic goods themselves.[51] Indeed, in various forms throughout their work, Finnis and Grisez suggest that moral choices are those which remain open to all the basic goods, that moral choices cannot be moral and act against a basic good.[52] Beyond these constraints of choice, however, no intrinsic order or hierarchy shapes the set of goods;

the authors argue that the basic goods are among themselves "incommensurable" and heterogeneous[53] (the claim resembles Nussbaum's description of the heterogeneous nature of goods in the world).

Finnis and Grisez's ethical view offers much of interest and much to contest.[54] Several obvious problems bear upon my own concerns as they will emerge in my exegesis of Aquinas. To begin with, the rejection of teleology sets Finnis and Grisez in clear opposition to Aquinas, who begins the prima secundae of his *Summa* with a dialectical treatment of the human end.[55] His core definitions of natural law rest on the claim of human directedness to "connatural" goods.[56] Without teleology, the natural law would be without function, could not be at all as Thomas defines it. But this remark cannot serve as in itself an objection to Finnis and Grisez: they have certainly given up any claim that their natural law is Aquinas's. Still, one might push the question of teleology in a way that strikes them closer to home. How is it that they can endorse their set of basic human goods by claiming that they are desired, self-evidently, by human beings, and yet disclaim any teleology? They seem to imply a kind of directedness to human desires that is very much bound up with Thomas's teleological exposition of the natural law.

Indeed, Finnis and Grisez's persistence in calling their moral theory *natural law* seems either sentimental, a nostalgic acknowledgment of the philosophical home they have departed, or inconsistent. Natural law as a theory carries with it the presumption that nature is in some sense normative for human action. Their use of the term seems inconsistent insofar as they appeal to "natural dispositions" to ground their claims about basic goods and yet disclaim the authority of teleology for them. Finnis and Grisez defend this move by saying that "human fulfillment" is neither "found" from a kind of theoretical diagram of a *telos* nor improvised without constraints. This may be true, but why they believe that teleology must be construed in such crude terms is unclear. They also believe themselves obligated to divorce themselves from teleological claims because of their adherence to the ought/is separation, which again seems precisely inimical to any authentic doctrine of natural law.

The formality of the Finnis-Grisez definition of practical reason is ultimately very limiting. I wish to offer a view of practical reason that allows for more-than-formal criteria in assessing the rightness of choices.[57] In this regard, prudence will be necessary both for practical understanding of the human good and for finding the means to achieve that good. This will take us well beyond the formality of Finnis and Grisez's criteria. The claims that Aquinas makes regarding human goods emerge from a philosophical view of human nature and human flourishing. This to my mind is no worse, and indeed may be better, than grounding such claims in self-evidence. Claims of self-evidence are notoriously vulnerable to objection, and the self-evidence of the basic goods enumerated by Finnis and Grisez is no less questionable. It is unclear, from the peremptoriness with which the goods are offered as basic, how one might determine, from various alternative basic goods, which are genuinely basic and which derivative.

I will in large part put aside the natural law theory of John Finnis and Germain Grisez. I do not deem it a bona fide theory of natural law, and their differences with Aquinas are so extensive that a wholesale examination of those differences could be undertaken only as a separate project of its own.

Nelson:
Prudence Unguided

Lastly, it will be helpful to examine a recent book on Thomistic ethics, Daniel Mark Nelson's *The Priority of Prudence*.[58] Nelson begins with some of the preoccupations of my own study. He notes the presence in Aquinas's ethics of the standards both of virtue and of the natural law.[59] He repudiates conventional legalistic interpretations of Aquinas, and he rightly insists on the importance in Thomistic ethics of the moral virtues and, especially, of prudence.[60] Nelson repeatedly emphasizes the epistemic problems involved in claims of knowledge of the natural law; these problems emerge in his characterization of the standard conception of natural law as the timeless, independent, universal, and absolute "higher law."... Natural law underlies, justifies, and also judges all human law, morality, and institutions.... [I]t is ordinarily presented as a deductive system in which conclusions in the form of specific moral judgments are derived from premises, a hierarchy of fundamental principles grounded in an essential human nature.[61]

Against this view, Nelson argues for the primacy in Aquinas of prudence and the virtues over the natural law.

One looks to the accumulated moral wisdom and the habitual behavior and judgments of virtuous individuals in one's community as the basic source of information about the rightness or wrongness of human action. Natural law functions theologically to explain how the world, created by a rational and purposive God, contains as much agreement about virtue as it does, but natural law is not a source of moral information specific enough to be immediately useful for guiding conduct.[62]

I will argue in the chapters to come for an interpretation of Thomas that integrates the standards of prudence and the natural law. For natural law to function effectively as a standard, prudence must operate on the communal and individual levels. But for prudence to operate effectively, the *inclinationes* must come into play—those specific directednesses that are the core of the natural law for Aquinas.[63] Without acknowledgment of this teleology, one cannot locate in Aquinas any notion of natural human flourishing. Without such a notion, prudence does not have an end to deliberate towards; it has of course the particulars of each situation, but the particulars acquire the significance prudence gives them only in light of the question, How can this serve to help achieve the human end?[64] Nelson neglects adequate treatment of the natural human end (although he does acknowledge God as ultimate end).[65] But, as I will argue, human prudence cannot steer itself by referring to God as ultimate end, since this is an end of which we do not have sufficient apprehension here and now.[66]

Prudence's need for a natural notion of human flourishing is precisely what Nelson omits in his account of Aquinas's ethics.

In turn this ellipsis produces certain distortions in what he represents as Thomas's ethics. The natural law for Aquinas is far more than, as Nelson asserts, a way of "talking about how it is that we act at all";[67] likewise, it does far more than "functio[n] formally to account for the judgements of prudence."[68] The *inclinationes* provide direction and guidance for the deliberations of prudence; they provide the basis for our knowledge of our natural good. While, to be sure, we cannot adequately know what our good is, independently of prudence, still prudence does not operate alone. In this regard, Nelson falls prey to some of the crude characterizations of the natural lawyers he criticizes. He correctly rejects claims of "natural knowledge" of the natural law, whether such claims rely on some brand of intuitionism or on deductive knowledge of right action independent of prudence. But more is left than the alternative that natural law is only a formal explanation for action.[69] Natural law, as Thomas's way of describing the teleology of our natures towards our natural good, provides a ground for the virtues and part of the matter about which prudence deliberates.

My account of Aquinas is distinguished from Nelson's in at least two other important respects. First, I present the natural law and prudence as themselves only fully intelligible when supplemented by human and then divine law. Natural law must be further determined by human law to be efficacious on the political level.[70] And the divine law is also required—both to correct for the effects of sin (which involves loss of our knowledge of the natural law) and to make possible union with God, the ultimate human end. In relation to the divine law, I will discuss sin, the need for grace, and the New Law. In providing this discussion, I will also note some features in Aquinas of the historical or narrative development of our knowledge of the human good.[71]

Nelson attempts to limit his examination of natural law and prudence to the natural level, in isolation from their ultimately theological context. Nelson's account then appears as an odd amalgam: an attempt to treat of the operation of prudence without adequate acknowledgment of the natural human end, and an acknowledgment of the human ultimate end, God, without discussion of the means to it.

Distortions of understanding of Thomas's ethics can arise from failure to grasp that natural law, the virtues (natural and theological), and divine law function together within his teleological ethics. Each of the philosophers I have discussed in this chapter has failed to understand Aquinas in this regard. Strauss, Jaffa, Nussbaum, and Goerner all express dissatisfaction with the standard of law in ethics: it is inflexible, good only for the most part, inferior to the standard of prudence. Strauss, Jaffa, and Nussbaum criticize Thomas for excessive legalism; Goerner vindicates Thomas only by locating within his ethics the standard of prudence itself. Nelson misunderstands Aquinas by construing the natural law in essentially formal terms; this leaves prudence with inadequate deliberative guidance. Finnis and Grisez, in constructing their own version of natural law, reject teleology altogether.

In what follows, we will see that, for Aquinas, the natural law functions as a guide for action only with the assistance of prudence; likewise, prudence relies on the natural law to furnish a natural standard of human flourishing. Far from being incompatible, the standards of prudence and the natural law prove to be interdependent.

2. NATURAL LAW AS LAW

Thomas discusses law in a number of his writings. I am going to consider only the assertions and arguments of the *Summa theologiae*. I have chosen to draw exclusively from the *Summa theologiae* in making my arguments in part for its chronological placement: it may represent the most mature work of Thomas on the law and the virtues. But chiefly I focus my study on the *Summa* because of the clarity and comprehensiveness of its treatment of law, of the virtues, and of related topics. What in fact Thomas does in the *Summa* is to connect all of his ethical teaching with its necessary ontological supports. The very structure of the *Summa* itself, dialectical in nature, hinges on the relationship and interdependence of its many parts.[1] To draw on this text in a conscientious way requires the tracing of connections among different parts of Thomas's argument. In the chapters that follow I try to display some of those connections.

Many of the commentators of whom I took note in the first chapter identify Thomistic natural law with a set of precepts and prohibitions, with an ethical standard of rules. Strauss, Nussbaum, and Jaffa indict the inflexibility of such a standard; Goerner tries to interpret the natural law on an analogy with human law. But in fact the natural law is linked time and again, within that section of the *Summa* designated as treating of laws, with eternal law, by which God governs the entire cosmos. Making good sense of this claim will enable us better to locate the distortions in the interpretations of Strauss, Goerner, and the rest. It will also help us to spell out the links between the natural law and the work of (human) prudence. In order to appreciate what the eternal law is for Thomas, however, we must begin in the prima pars of the *Summa theologiae.*

Providence and Rational Creatures

Early in the prima pars of the *Summa*, within an inquiry about the divine attributes, Thomas discusses the nature of God's providence.[2] Thomas argues that ascribing providence to God is fitting because goodness is found in creatures not only in their "substance" but also insofar as they are ordered to their "ultimate end, which is divine goodness."[3] God is himself the cause of the directedness in things, and the *ratio,* idea, of this effect preexists in the divine intellect. The *ratio* of this form of directedness in creatures is what Aquinas calls divine providence. He immediately continues:

> [Providence] is the principal part of prudence, to which the other two parts are ordered, namely, memory of what is past and understanding of the present. Insofar as it is from the memory of the past, and from the understanding of the present, that we infer (*conjectamus*) how to provide for the future.[4]

Thomas treats providence in its literal sense as a kind of foresight (and consequently preparation for what is foreseen). While God is himself not ordered to an end, his ordering of creatures to himself is, Thomas argues, a kind of prudence. The directedness of creatures pertains to their future, both in terms of time as well as their development. Thus to ascribe providence to God is appropriate.

Thomas goes on to argue for the unfailing subjection of all things to God's providence.[5] He distinguishes the way in which providence operates with regard to nonrational creatures from the manifestation of divine providence in rational creatures. But God does not determine human beings to one end, as he does nonrational natural things. Rather, rational creatures "direct themselves to an end . . . through free will, because they can take counsel and they can choose."[6] Since God is the very cause of free will, all effects of human free will are still subject to divine providence: "Human providence is contained under the providence of God, as a particular cause under a universal cause."[7]

Thomas does not in this discussion spell out fully the precise way in which human providence operates in relation to the providence of God; neither does he spell out how men and women are directed to their ultimate end. The secunda pars itself undertakes to describe human beings and how they, with intellect and will, both direct themselves and, in doing so, return to God. In his prologue to the prima secundae, Thomas cites John Damascene to emphasize the connections between the secunda pars of the *Summa* and what has preceded it.

> As the Damascene says, man is said to be made in the image of God, as *image* signifies an intellectual being, with free will and power over himself; so, since we have spoken about the exemplar, God, and about those things which proceed from the divine power according to his will, it remains for us to consider God's image, which is man, according to which he is also the principle of his own works, having free will and power over his acts.[8]

So, Thomas says, we will examine human beings on an analogy with God, since they resemble God in very precise ways (intellect, will, the power of self-direction). But Thomas will be attentive as well in placing restrictions on the analogy, and not merely by expressing the limitations of rational creatures in comparison to the infinite God. Thomas carefully draws in the analogy by bringing human self-direction, call it human prudence, under the prudence of God. He has of course asserted this subordination in the prima pars of the *Summa*, in the passage examined above; he will unpack and enrich the claim within the secunda pars.

Let me make some brief remarks regarding the structure of the secunda pars itself, up to what is popularly called the Treatise on Law (a designation not originating with Aquinas himself). In the secunda pars, Thomas begins with an inquiry into the human end, for which no natural good or set of goods can suffice (q. 1–5); only God, as known and loved in the beatific vision, can fully satisfy the human appetites for truth and good.[9] He then takes

up an examination of action, including a discussion of the will
(q. 6–17), of the criteria for good and bad action (q. 18–21), and
of the emotions (q. 22–48). Thomas proceeds to a treatment of
the virtues, both natural and theological (q. 49–70).

At this stage of the prima secundae, the dialectical structure of
the topics addressed resembles the structure of the *Nicomachean
Ethics*. Both Aristotle and Thomas deem it necessary to resolve
first the issue of the human *telos*; Aristotle also discusses vol-
untariness, and his claims about the virtues incorporate remarks
on the passions as their ground. Perhaps Aristotle is Thomas's
chief interlocutor in the secunda pars, just as Pseudo-Dionysus
is in the prima pars. Thomas's appropriation and correction of
Aristotle I will address further on. It suffices now to point out
that already Thomas establishes differences with Aristotle in his
own characterization of God as the human end, and in how
he organizes the virtues as either acquired (natural) or infused
(theological). Aristotle of course does not recognize the latter
category, and indeed Thomas's configuration of even the natural
virtues will show the effects of his acknowledgment of faith, hope,
and charity.

Aquinas's differences with Aristotle seem to deepen as we push
further into the prima secundae. After his first treatment of the
virtues comes a lengthy discussion of sin and its kinds, degrees,
and effects (q. 71–89). Immediately following his discourse on
sin is his treatment of law (q. 90–114). As we will see, by no
accident does a discourse on law ensue upon one on sin. Thomas
has asserted, in the prima pars, the unfailing nature of God's
providence, which can be easily seen in the determination of
the behavior of nonrational creatures. More needs to be said
about rational creatures, not only because they have free will
but also because they abuse this freedom (in sin). Thus Aquinas
must account for how human self-direction still falls under God's
own governance of the cosmos; he also, in the light of his own
claims about human sinfulness, must account for how God's
providence prevails even in men and women who turn away from
it. (Goerner's remarks on the Germans will prove helpful here.)

Law and Its Kinds

We can now proceed to take up the first part (q. 90–97) of Thomas's examination of law. In his prologue to this section, he characterizes his treatment of laws as part of a treatment of the "exterior principle" moving us to good, namely, God, who "instructs us through law and helps us through grace."[10] The Treatise on Law specifically addresses both law and grace. The nature of law's "instruction" bears directly upon the function of the natural law for rational creatures.

Thomas begins with a basic definition of law. Law is rational (*aliquid rationis*), directed to the common good by a person or persons responsible for a community, and promulgated adequately.[11] Thomas distinguishes four kinds of law: eternal law, natural law, human law, and divine law. But these are not species of law of equivalent authority and domain: eternal law is clearly the core form of law, from which all other forms derive.[12] Indeed, natural law, human law, and divine law all pertain to rational creatures and how they stand with respect to eternal law, the law by which God governs the cosmos.[13] Natural, human, and divine law, working together, are how eternal law is manifested in and for rational creatures. With these three forms of law Thomas resolves the problem he set for himself in the prima pars and in the earlier portions of the prima secundae: How does God's providence extend to free and rational creatures? How does it extend to human beings bearing the consequences of sin?

Note that how eternal law is characterized links it directly with God's providential direction of the cosmos. In his first treatment of eternal law, Thomas says that eternal law is the *ratio* in God of his governance of the cosmos.[14] This is the precise way in which divine providence has been described in the prima pars. In the question designated for the discussion of eternal law in itself, Thomas elaborates on his claim by speaking of God as creator as well as governor of the cosmos. There preexist in the divine mind "ideas" which are God's conceptions both of everything that is made and of the order of all creation.

So the idea (*ratio*) of divine wisdom, moving all things to their due end, possesses the *ratio* of law; and in accordance with this the eternal law is nothing other than the *ratio* of divine wisdom, which directs all actions and motions.[15]

Thomas goes on to argue for the subjection of all creation to the eternal law,[16] which brings us to rational creatures and how they stand with respect to this unfailing law for creatures.

Natural Law and Eternal Law

The natural law is how divine providence is exercised with regard to rational creatures; it is, Thomas says, the rational creature's "participation" in eternal law.[17] What does Thomas mean when he speaks of our "participation" in eternal law? Natural law, he says, is what orders us to our "proper act and end" by natural inclination.[18] Whatever else it involves, natural law is primarily how we are directed to our end, which is ultimately God. "For among others, the rational creature is subject to divine providence in a more excellent way, inasmuch as it is itself a sharer (*particeps*) in providence, being provident for itself and for others."[19] Thomas indicates here that the directedness of natural law is not coercive or without sense for the rational creature; Thomas has called the guidance law gives "instruction,"[20] and he claims that the "light of natural reason," permitting us knowledge of good and evil, so instructs us in natural law.[21] He then very clearly establishes a link between our possession of the natural law (in terms of our being directed to our proper end), and our knowledge of that directedness (which in turn provides criteria for good and evil in action). Thomas's own emphasis on the natural law is first in terms of *inclinationes*, ways of being directed to our end, and not in terms of any set of rules. His related point of emphasis is how the natural law requires, in ways that will be spelled out, the free and responsible exercise of intellect and will. Thus human self-direction is not simply overridden by it.

Thomas's characterization of our participation in eternal law as a kind of instruction or education is intended to fulfill the

requirement that all law, even eternal law, be promulgated in the
proper way. The natural law succeeds in promulgation because,
he says, "God puts it into men's minds to be known naturally."[22]
What is known, and how it is known, requires the exercise of
both intellect and will. To be instructed in the natural law, we
must engage in a kind of practical reasoning that is itself both
self-education and self-discovery.[23]

It is clear from how Thomas speaks of natural law that it
comprises principally forms of directedness towards our proper
ends or goods. Moreover, if one takes the rational character of
this law seriously, then natural law also affords us understanding
of the goods to which we are so directed. We must see and
assent to pursue in specific ways the goods to which we are
inclined by our natures. The eternal law is also for rational and
nonrational creatures forms of determination or directedness to
an end; but rational creatures recognize their *inclinationes* for what
they are, as law, while "irrational creatures are under eternal
law insofar as they are moved by divine providence but not
through understanding of the divine precepts, as with rational
creatures."[24]

In this sense, knowledge of the natural law clearly is meant to
have some of the components of prudence, which also enables
the appraisal and recognition of certain ends as good.[25] But
to recognize the goods to which we are ordered is not necessarily to recognize in concrete ways what we should or should
not do to attain those goods. For an understanding of what takes
place in that kind of practical reasoning, we must look at natural
law in more detail.

In question 94 of the prima secundae, Thomas discusses natural law and its most fundamental characteristics. He begins with
a description of how natural law is a habit;[26] it is a *habitus*
insofar as we hold the fundamental principles of this law by
the habit of *synderesis.* These principles form the core knowledge
of natural law within us, and these principles, held by *synderesis,*
are "indelible," persisting in even the most vicious.[27] Practical
reason pertains to action, and so its first principles must pertain
to what is to be sought or avoided within action.

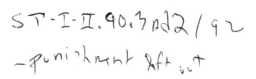

[S]o good is what first falls under the apprehension of the practical reason, which is ordered to action, since every agent acts for an end which has the aspect (*ratio*) of a good. Therefore, the first principle in the practical reason is what is founded on the *ratio* of good, which is: good is what all things desire. Hence this is the first precept of law, that good is to be done and pursued, and evil is to be avoided.[28]

Every rational creature, Aquinas says, has this much of an apprehension of good and evil, even infants and the damned.[29] Thus neither developed cognitive abilities nor the moral clarity given by the virtues would seem to be required for the possession of *synderesis*. The understanding it affords is on an analogy with the first principle of speculative reason (the principle of noncontradiction), says Thomas.[30] Just as one cannot think intelligibly without upholding the truth that something cannot be and not be at the same time in the same way, so one cannot act intelligibly, i.e., deliberately and rationally, without acting purposively, for the sake of some end understood as good. Teleology of this most general kind underlies all the more specific and substantive *inclinationes* of the natural law for Aquinas.

In this respect, Thomas claims that *synderesis* is infallible,[31] although application of its principles can be in error. I understand by this claim of infallibility a fundamental link between *synderesis* and what Thomas says regarding the will—that it chooses always under the formal aspect of goodness, the *ratio boni*.[32]

The function of *synderesis* is conceptual, determining how we consider, in practical reasoning, actions, choices, objects of desire, i.e., in terms of goods and evils. *Synderesis* secures us accessibility to the notions of good and evil within reasoning about action. Of course, much more than *synderesis* is required to determine the right application of these notions.[33] We can be mistaken about what is the good for us and about how to achieve it. Knowledge of such matters requires deliberation and reflection; we do not arrive at answers by immediate apprehension (as Daniel Mark Nelson correctly argued). The first principle of practical reason does not then yield specific knowledge of genuine goods; it provides only

the most general way to characterize the end of an action: as
a good, as something to be desired. Indeed, Thomas casts the
understanding of good given within *synderesis* as "good is what
all things desire." This is a statement of teleology on the most
universal level; there is not even reference to what is specific to
human desire for the good.

Why then is *synderesis* so important for Aquinas? A Neopla-
tonic concept within Aquinas's largely Aristotelian epistemology,
its presence seems therefore problematic and has certainly vexed
Thomas's defenders to nightmare.[34] The importance of *synderesis*,
on my view, springs from the starting point that it provides
for any inquirer in the moral life. Given this capacity, an agent
cannot completely lack guidance in the moral life. He or she
has even initially some root, inerrant apprehension of the good
with which to begin the moral life and moral deliberation. We
begin with at least the necessary conceptual equipment. *Synderesis*
provides the most basic tutelage in reasoning about action; it
secures, infallibly, that the right questions will be asked, that
actions will be reasoned about under the descriptions of good
or evil.[35]

Indeed *synderesis*, together with the *inclinationes* that are the
primary constituents of the natural law, guides deliberation about
the human good. The habit of *synderesis* alone is by no means
sufficient for ethical guidance. The forms of directedness give
practical content to the conceptual apprehensions of good and
evil provided by *synderesis*; they specify what is meant by *good* in
terms of human flourishing. Thus there are on Aquinas's view
activities and states which are naturally desired by men and
women as goods. This much can be counted on no matter to
what sort of human community one belongs. Such seems to be
Thomas's claim when he says that the natural law, in its most
general (*communissima*) principles, is known to all and cannot
be erased from the human heart.[36] Insofar as one is speaking of
rational creatures, one is speaking of beings with intellect and
will, and with a set of *inclinationes* that constitute in part the
natural law for them. It still remains for them to reflect upon
the *inclinationes*, to reflect upon the goods constitutive of their

flourishing, in order to derive more specific rules for conduct. To
this we now turn.

Thomas speaks of natural law's primary precepts, which pertain to the goods to which our inclinations direct us by nature
(this is the primary sense of *natural law* for Aquinas).

> Thus it is that all those things to which man has a natural incli-
> nation, reason naturally apprehends as goods and consequently
> as things to be pursued, and their contraries as evil, and things
> to be avoided. Therefore the order of the precepts of the natural
> law is according to the order of natural inclinations.[37]

In this secondary sense of natural law, the sense of its rules, there
are three sets of precepts.[38] These correspond to the hierarchy
of the *inclinationes* themselves. The first set of precepts guides
the preservation of human life, a good which we share with all
living things. The second set pertains to the begetting and rearing
of offspring, goods which we share with other animals. Third
are precepts that govern the goods to which humans incline as
specifically rational beings; Thomas mentions in particular our
desire "to know the truth about God and to live in society."[39]

In so sketching the goods to which we are ordered naturally,
Thomas presents us with a natural human end which is "inclusive," not "monolithic."[40] Our happiness is achieved in a number
of activities—in health-sustaining physical activity, in constituting
and sustaining the goods of family life, in the conversations and
pleasures of good friendships, in meaningful participation in civic
activities, and, to the degree to which we are able naturally, in rational activity yielding knowledge about God.[41] But this inclusive
natural end is also hierarchical in the structure of its constituent
goods: Thomas speaks of the "order" of precepts following the
"order" of natural inclinations. Those goods to which we are
inclined as rational creatures have greatest value.[42] Among these,
knowledge about God, even within the limited reach of natural
contemplation, is the highest and best good. But rational activity
also regulates the mode of enjoyment for lesser goods: the goods
which we share with other animals and with all living things are
to be enjoyed in a specifically rational way. In this way they are
constituents of the human end.[43]

In his core treatment of the contents of the natural law, Aquinas does not so much as spell out some of the actual rules of the natural law. Instead, he is concerned with establishing a fundamental link between any precept of the natural law and the goods to which the precepts are ordered. Thomas does not here tell us which rules are necessary for human beings to achieve the good of living in society; he tells us that some rules will be necessary to this end. Thus the characterization by many philosophers of *not* Thomas as a legalist and of his natural law as chiefly rule oriented *light* does not stand up to a careful reading of the text.

In what way are the actual precepts arrived at? What are their contents? Such rules involve an articulation of which actions are conducive towards, or destructive of, those goods to which our *inclinationes* direct us. That is, through individual and social reflection, we may come to understand what actions promote attainment of our good and what actions damage or destroy attainment. We may then express this understanding, and render it practically efficacious, through the formulation of rules prescribing or proscribing certain actions. Such rules articulate further what we mean by good and evil; they encourage acts ordered to the attainment of flourishing and discourage acts destructive of flourishing. As such, the rules enrich the conceptual apprehensions of good and evil that are afforded by *synderesis*. They may also enrich our understanding of the forms of directedness themselves insofar as they specify what is minimally necessary to attain the goods of our nature. Indeed, observance of these precepts may in part constitute the goods to which we are directed (as they can be achieved in specific communities).

The last three articles of question 94 address the issue of human knowledge of the natural law. Thomas stresses the unalterability of the natural law at its core; he also specifies the range of impediments to clear knowledge of this law. In discussing both concerns, Aquinas again makes clear how much knowledge of, and obedience to, the natural law requires the careful exercise of practical reason. In arguing for a unitary natural law for all, Thomas explains some of the difficulties of reasoning from general principles to concrete, specific applications of the principle. The nature of practical reasoning will produce variation in conclusions, as well as in apprehension of these conclusions, of the natural law.

But as far as the proper conclusions of practical reason, neither is truth or rectitude the same for all, nor even when it is the same, is it equally known. Thus it is right and true that all act according to reason, and from this principle it follows as a proper conclusion that deposits [or belongings] should be returned. Now this is true in most cases, but it could happen that in some case it would be harmful, and consequently unreasonable, if deposits were returned: suppose that someone sought to attack one's own country [with the returned goods]. And this principle will be found to fail the more it descends into particulars.[44]

Aquinas demonstrates how general principles can fail because of the specific circumstances of a special case: it would in fact be wrong to return what was owed where what was returned would be used to harmful purpose. Practical reasoning about the good here and now (that is to say, prudence) must decide how to fit the general principle to the particular circumstance. This will not be done with equal adeptness by all: what is required is the ability both to grasp the relevant particulars of the situation and to understand what the point of the general principle is, what the good is at which the principle aims. In the example of practical reasoning just quoted, I think it is clear that Aquinas is at best sketching the stages of the reasoning involved. "Act according to reason" may admit of further amplification before reaching "Return what has been loaned." Clearly, his own conception of the precepts of the natural law is very far indeed from a mechanical, legalistic conception of morality. Without the exercise of prudential judgment in amplifying, and then applying, the natural law, the law could not be a workable guide to action.

Thomas does not stop at showing the way in which general precepts can fail in particular applications. He also asserts that knowledge of the natural law can fail, even though it is possessed by every rational creature. He states that there can be effective impediments to our knowledge (*notitia*) or awareness of the natural law. Our reason can become distorted (*depravata*) by passion, by evil custom, or by evil disposition of nature.[45] It is in this regard that Thomas cites the Germans, who failed to recognize the natural-law prohibition against robbery. Thomas returns to this point in article 6, explaining that the most general principles of the natural law cannot be obscured, but they can be blocked in their application, by excess of passion, for example. Just so, secondary, i.e., more derivative, precepts can be wiped out (*deleri*) by "evil customs and corrupt habits."[46]

As Goerner implies in his own discussion of the Germans, Thomas's conception of the natural law is fraught with an awareness of human life in its social and historical forms. On Thomas's own view, it is part of our *inclinationes* that we live in community. The forms of community in which we participate, and in which we are educated, will then have serious consequences for the extent of our practical reasoning's excellence (understanding such reasoning as drawing on knowledge of the goods to which we are directed by the natural law). That is to say, not even natural law can escape the impact of individual and social practice and history. Rather, knowledge of the natural law may be either nurtured or stifled through particular cultural forms and social practices. Cultural forms and practices are important in two ways to the natural law as I characterize it here. First, achievement of the goods to which we are directed naturally can occur in a variety of configurations and forms, as Thomas seems to recognize by his characterization of the need for amplification of the natural law in its most general precepts, including the further specification provided by human law (as I will discuss below). There are simply different ways to achieve the goods of family, friendship, intellectual inquiry, and so forth; a diversity of ways of achievement can exist within a society (and other ways may exist in other societies).[47]

This claim permits, even requires, that particular cultural forms and institutions be subject themselves to criticism and revision. Revision would occur if such forms and expressions were deemed damaging to human flourishing per se. Understanding of flourishing must be, on Thomas's terms, mediated by social practice and history but cannot be wholly determined by it. If it were so determined, no progress in knowledge of our good could occur either by new discovery or by correction. Thus this interpretation of the natural law does not at all conflate with the natural law tradition or long custom: witness the Germans' long-standing, but, on Thomas's view, still corrupt, practice of raiding. I will discuss in the last chapter how the Germans might be understood to have learned the natural law with regard to robbery. In the next chapter, we will examine how the Old Law helped the Jewish community to relearn the natural law. Both stories illustrate eventual progress in knowledge of the natural law within specific communities.

Secondly, cultural forms and practices are relevant to the natural law insofar as they may help or hinder knowledge of the means to the goods of human life. Thomas clearly indicates that epistemic blocks to such knowledge can occur through the moral obscurity inflicted by vice or excess passion. We can lose knowledge of the natural law as we lose active orientation to the goods of our nature. Social forms and practices can help produce forgetfulness of the natural law by promoting (or failing to curb) unruly passion or by expressing an inversion of the natural hierarchy of goods (as in the communal practice of idolatry).[48] Social practices are subject to criticism on the basis of, once again, their tendency to promote or hinder flourishing, including whether they work for or against the acquisition of the virtues. Social forms and history are thus necessary for expressing a community's understanding of what human flourishing is and for promoting knowledge and practice of the means to those goods. Indeed, it may sometimes be difficult to distinguish in fact between what practices express a community's understanding of flourishing and what practices promote attainment of it.

The Argument So Far

God orders all creatures in a way appropriate to their various natures by the eternal law. For rational creatures (made in God's image), this ordering must be in keeping with their special dignity as beings with intellect and will. Thomas calls natural law the rational creature's way of partaking in eternal law. This partaking occurs in human beings' directedness to specific goods by their nature. But men and women also partake in the eternal law by their knowledge and choice: (1) they must recognize certain *inclinationes* as normative, as ordering them toward specific goods; and (2) they must discover and choose the means by which they can achieve the goods to which they are so directed.

Natural law is not a theoretical knowledge of propositions; rather, it is a possession of ends and of ways of discovering means to those ends.[49] Our discovery of the natural law occurs by way of reflection upon our natures and then by discovery of the necessary means for achieving or constituting the goods of our natures. These means include the formation of rules to help secure and constitute the good for us. We both give the law to ourselves and discover it.

This discovery, I stress, takes place within a life, within the narrative context of experiences that engage a person's intellect and will in the making of concrete choices.[50] In attention to what makes up one's experience and in the making of choices, both good and bad, a human being augments understanding of his or her own nature and of what most promotes the flourishing of that nature. This process of inquiry is, then, one of practical reasoning, practical reasoning which must be carried on individually and communally. And in so mentioning practical reasoning, the operation of some measure of prudential deliberation is implied.[51]

Such an understanding of natural law at least escapes the pitfalls of treating the rules of the natural law as though they were intuitively knowable or evident through reason operating a priori: the process I am describing would be far more rough-and-ready, also far more historical. Discovery takes time. If we eventually arrive at some knowledge of self-evident truths, it will only be through the laborious acquisition of them through reflection on our experience.

This account of natural law also emphasizes its rational character, while at the same time not reducing natural law merely to propositional knowledge. We participate in eternal law by the experiencing of directedness to ends and by the possession of capacities for finding means to those ends.[52] Only by the free exercise of our practical rationality could we discover the natural law so understood, and this discovery would involve in part doing over again the work of the first legislator, God.[53] In that sense, God first manifests his providence through the eternal law (in which natural law participates), and so directs all creatures to himself. Just so, men and women imitate (and yet obey) divine providence by directing themselves in discovering and pursuing their good. They follow divine providence by being provident for themselves. Indeed, this renders more intelligible Aquinas's claim, earlier in the *Summa*, that human prudence is included within the providence of God.[54]

An understanding of particular rules of the natural law, e.g., "Never murder,"[55] is inseparable from an understanding of the rules' point and purpose, on Aquinas's view. One cannot reason down to specific cases without some apprehension of the goal of a precept. To attempt to do so would be to separate the rules from their real function: to help secure the goods of human life. What the prohibition against murder prevents is the kind of disrespect for human life that would be destructive of life in community; without this law, a community could not exist in such a way as to pursue the various goods constitutive of social life.

And only prudence can give such an understanding of the end or purpose of law, on the Aristotelian and the Thomistic views. Thus to divorce natural law from the virtues is to misunderstand how both the law and the virtues alike conduce human beings to their proper goods. It would also be to misunderstand how one arrives at the specific rules of the natural law in the first place. Given that only prudence can yield a realization of the ends we pursue as genuine goods, it seems it must operate in the discovery of the natural law.[56]

Prudence and Its Work

I have made repeated reference to prudence within my account of the natural law. I now will sketch Thomas's own description of it, in part to show its function with the natural law. Thomas states that prudence is in the cognitive faculty; it is of the practical, not the speculative, reason.[57] The exercise of prudence yields knowledge of a certain kind, and it reasons about action to be performed towards an end. It is not in us by nature, except in its most universal principles, but is developed through "discovery by way of experience or by learning."[58] It pertains to the knowledge of singulars.[59] Thomas's description is Aristotelian in many respects, stressing prudence's deliberative, means-finding function and its attention to particulars. But he also, very quietly within his exposition, reformulates prudence in the light of the natural law's role of directing us to the good.

In the same article that states prudence's need to know particulars, Thomas interjects that the prudent person must know both the "universal principles of reason" as well as particulars. This formulation is very similar to how Thomas has spoken of the most general principles of the natural law.[60] He makes prudence's link to the natural law even plainer in a discussion of prudence and the moral virtues.

Aquinas begins by claiming that the moral virtues set the end for prudence.[61] This is what we would expect him to say, following Aristotle. But Thomas goes on to state that prudence relates to synderesis: "Natural reason determines the ends of the moral virtues by what is called synderesis."[62] Thus prudence ultimately takes its goals from synderesis; indeed, as he amplifies later, prudence reasons from synderesis, "just as understanding of [first] principles moves scientific knowledge."[63] Here he seems to me to suggest that prudence involves insight into synderesis even as it reasons from it; our understanding of first principles is enriched in scientific inquiry. Just so, our synderetic grasp of good and evil is enriched in practical inquiry and pursuit of actual goods. We may actually augment our understanding of the first principles of action by building up more extensive knowledge of what good and evil are for us. We begin with "natural" knowledge of good and evil in synderesis but further that knowledge by a deliberative prudence working upon the matter of our desires and choices.

Prudence on this view functions, even in imperfect exercise, within our discovery of the natural law and the goods to which it directs us. Just so, it helps to generate the very rules (of the natural law) that it will then work to apply and extend. For no rule, let alone those of the natural law, can be applied or constituted without an accompanying understanding of the rules' point as understood by prudence. This is so because to know how to apply a rule or even to know which rule to apply requires the exercise of practical judgment; such judgment would have to pick out of the situation at hand the relevant particulars in order to know which rule is appropriate for it. For example, even applying a rule as absolute as the prohibition against murder requires some grasp of what constitutes murder and a grasp of which situations fall under that prohibition.[64] One cannot intelligently select and apply a rule without some (prudential) grasp of the good that the rule is seeking to secure or protect. And some rules must be exceptionless, for example the rule against murder, because certain goods are so crucial for an attainment of our end and because certain actions, such as murder, operate so unequivocally to destroy these goods.

One further aspect of prudence I would like to draw out. In speaking of the "quasi-integral," i.e., constitutive, parts of prudence, Aquinas lists eight such parts: memory, understanding (*intellectus*, corresponding to *nous* in Greek), docility or teach-ableness, ingeniousness (*solertia*), reason, foresight (*providentia*), circumspection (vigilance as to right means), and caution (against obstacles).[65] This is certainly a conscientious reconciliation of authorities' opinions on prudence. Yet the catalogue shows for prudence not only the need for deliberative skills but also an experience-gathering requirement that acknowledges that both memory, involving recollection and reflection on the past, and foresight (*providentia*) are necessary for an accurate assessment of the present.[66] Thomas acknowledges, as in the case of our knowledge of the natural law, the developing and time-bound nature of prudence. In our casting back and forward in our experience we are best able to do justice to the present; we can as well acquire understanding of experience from others, who may serve as our teachers.[67]

Natural Law and Human Law

I have thus far spoken of our knowledge of the natural law aided by prudence as a knowledge which is progressive and historical; we work to acquire understanding of our natures, and of the means for the flourishing of our natures, through a process of inquiry that goes on individually and communally. But in making this last point, I run the risk of treating natural law in isolation from another form of law from which it can never be wholly separate: human law. For human life is always lived in community, on Thomas's view, and thus the general principles of the natural law must be further articulated (and supplemented) according to the special needs of individual communities. Human law is the law of specific communities. All such law should be derived from the natural law, Thomas argues. That derivation can occur in two ways:

> in one way, as conclusions from principles; in another way, as determinations of certain generalities. The first way is similar to that by which demonstrative conclusions proceed from principles in the sciences. The second way is similar to that by which, in the arts, common forms are determined to a certain particular case.[68]

As an example of the way of conclusions from more general principles, Thomas offers the move from "Do harm to no one" to "Do not kill." As an example of the way of further specification, Thomas explains that while the natural law dictates that offenders should be punished, it does not say how; human law determines what punishment should be for particular crimes.

Thus it is always a mistake to speak of natural law by itself as a guide for action. On Thomas's view, human law, the law of actual communities, has the responsibility to restate and to specify further what the natural law teaches. Indeed, natural law serves as the standard of justice for those making civil law. Thomas states that human law in discord with the natural law is "a corruption of law."[69] To go against the natural law is to act against the human good. Thus, civil laws which are not ordered to the human good are, Aquinas says, more like "violence rather than laws."[70] Clearly natural law is intended to work always in tandem with human law in communities: all law is intended to make people good, Thomas says,[71] and both the natural law and human law command acts of all the virtues.[72]

In his treatment of the human law, Thomas again acknowledges the specific social forms of human life. Natural law does not work in isolation, as a generic and wholly adequate moral standard applied in the same way across all communities. Instead, natural law requires further specificity in order to be effective as a guide to right action; specificity is given in human law, as formulated by prudent legislators.

Let us summarize our findings about the natural law and its functions before we take up certain questions Thomas raises about its efficacy. Recall that, in the first chapter, Nussbaum and Goerner argued at length, although in different ways, for the incompatibility of prudence and the natural law. Both understood the natural law to be primarily a legal standard comprising absolute rules. I believe I have shown that this is not at all what natural law is for Aquinas. It is primarily our directedness to the goods of our human nature. It is, secondarily, rules for the attainment of those goods. The rules, which are findings of practical reasoning, can be codified and implemented in human law. Further, it cannot then be the case for Aquinas that prudence and the rules of the natural law operate independently of one another. Neither can it be the case that they are incompatible. We need practical wisdom in order to discover and apply the rules of the natural law; but we gain our knowledge of the goods to which these rules should conduce from our essential and dynamic directedness towards these goods (in the natural law). Martha Nussbaum, her emphasis on the virtues notwithstanding, fails to understand that the virtues themselves presuppose a fundamental orientation to the good. This orientation makes them means to, and also constitutive of, human flourishing.

This is simply how Aquinas understands the natural law, not in terms of a code of rules. Likewise, Nussbaum fails to see in what way rule following, even of the kind she criticizes, requires some measure of prudence. There cannot be blind, mechanistic legalism of the kind that she describes; any successful rule following requires a measure of understanding. To follow a rule requires that the rule follower understand the point of the rule; this understanding testifies to the possession of some measure of prudence. E. A. Goerner, although a more careful reader of Aquinas, in a vein similar to Nussbaum persistently characterizes natural law in terms of absolute rules; he thus also neglects the more fundamental form of natural law in the *inclinationes*. By this neglect, he then fails also to see how the natural law and prudence are interdependent. By too completely severing the natural law from prudence, he does more than badly misinterpret Aquinas: he makes it impossible to understand how the natural law could function as a pedagogical tool (which is precisely the role on which Goerner lays stress). Without some understanding of the goods to which they are inclined by their natures (which would be given in prudential reflection), the Germans could never learn to recognize as penalties the penalties from which they suffer for violation of the natural law. The natural law might be their scourge; it could never be their teacher.

Natural Law and the Need for Divine Law

I have spoken now of the natural law and of our progressive acquisition of knowledge of it. Knowledge of it is progressive (1) in our coming to understand more about our natures and (2) in our coming to understand what means to choose in constituting the flourishing of our natures. Thomas repeatedly indicates that our inquiry regarding the natural law takes place socially and over time. Such indications include how prudence, which requires experience, is necessary for knowledge of the natural law. It also includes his remarks about the Germans and how there can be cultural and moral impediments to our knowledge of the natural law; add to this the fact that human law is needed to articulate and specify the natural law for particular communities. As I argued above, citizens of communities will encounter present understandings of the natural law within the laws and social practices of their own societies.

But my account of ongoing acquisition of (our knowledge of) the natural law is too simple as it now stands. Thomas builds into his account of law a fourth type, which also is derived from the eternal law (divine providence) but stands in curious relationship to the natural law itself. This fourth type is the divine law, the law revealed by God. Revelation comes in two distinct parts, the Old Law and the New Law. Divine law is necessary, Thomas tells us, because natural law does not suffice to order us to God; although our *inclinationes* direct us to "connatural" goods, God alone can completely satisfy us, and he is utterly beyond the reach of our powers. Thus the divine law aids us so that we may attain God.[73]

Moreover, humankind suffers under the burden of sin, one manifestation of which Thomas also characterizes as a quasi-law.[74] The *lex fomitis* is the law of concupiscence (literally, the law of tinder or kindling—the fire in the flesh which is not completely subject to reason). It is a consequence of our primordial rejection of God, and the unruliness of our passions constitutes a further block to our pursuit of the good, even as understood in terms of the natural law. Thus our natural powers are not only limited; they are infirm. Divine law is necessary as a remedy for the effects of sin. Thomas thus stresses not only the general social and historical nature of our inquiry and pursuit of the good; he also indicates that there is one very specific community and history to which we all belong. We are all the children of Adam and Eve, and our history is located within salvation history. Examination of the divine law will help us to deepen our understanding of what inquiry about our good involves, on Thomas's view. It will also deepen our understanding of the social and historical aspects of this inquiry.

3. NATURAL LAW AND THE OLD LAW

Thomas builds into his account of the natural law an acknowledgment of its need to be developed and applied by the work of prudence; moreover, he describes how human law must further specify the general precepts of the natural law in guiding human behavior. But also built into the Thomistic account of the natural law is an acknowledgment of that law's own constitutive inadequacy or incompleteness.

Natural law, even with human law, is deemed insufficient for human needs. While speaking early on about the different kinds of law, Thomas treats of this insufficiency in terms of the need for a divine law.[1] He adduces four reasons for divine law, the first of which is perhaps the most basic:

> because through law human beings are directed in their proper acts in accordance with (in ordine) their ultimate end. And if indeed man were ordered only to such an end as did not exceed the proportion of his natural faculty, it would not have been necessary for man to have some directive on the part of his reason above the natural law and human law. . . . But because man is ordered to the end of eternal beatitude, which exceeds the proportion of his natural faculty, it was necessary that, above the natural and human law, he was directed to his end by a law given by God.[2]

Natural law directs human beings to a hierarchy of goods commensurate with human powers. It does indeed conduce toward union with God; and "knowledge about God," among the goods to which it orders men and women, is its highest end.[3] But the natural knowledge of God of which human beings are capable falls far below the intimate union with God that Aquinas describes as the fit ultimate human end. Thus another law is needed, a law that derives from God and makes human beings able to attain God.[4]

Natural law is, then, not merely too general or too inchoate to be, by itself, a wholly adequate guide for human beings. It does not suffice to deliver men and women to union with God. We can thus interpret Thomas's hierarchy of laws (eternal, natural, human, divine) in terms of their capacities to direct human beings to their ultimate end. Natural law is how we as rational creatures participate in eternal law. With the needed amplification of human law, it orders us to enjoy finite goods in a rational manner and to approach God to the degree to which our powers permit us. But this is not enough to satisfy us,[5] and for this reason God provides a law with the capacity to help us to our final end. Thus the divine law completes what the natural law intends.[6] But the connections between the natural law and the higher, the more complete, law cannot be represented in terms of simple addition or supplementation.

As I suggested at the close of the last chapter, Thomas must take into account, within his ethics, the effects of sin. The presence of sin renders the work of the divine law more complex and less straightforward; human powers cannot simply be augmented for union with God to be achieved. How sin impairs our pursuit of God, even according to our natural faculties, is addressed in Thomas's description of the work of the divine law. The effects of sin must be addressed here, at least implicitly, in order for Thomas to explain how the divine law provided a cure or corrective for these effects. Within his discussion of the Old Law (q. 98–105 of the prima secundae), Thomas raises compelling questions about the reliability of natural knowledge of our good, and he provides a kind of history of how, through sin, our knowledge became so unreliable. In doing so, he teaches us more about his understanding of the natural law and how that law can be learned—or forgotten.

The Old Law and the Natural Law

The Old Law, Thomas maintains, was intended to begin the historical process of repairing the effects of sin. That Thomas begins his treatment of the Old Law with the question of whether it was in fact good is thus startling and important.[7] The body of Thomas's response to the question bears upon how the Old Law led toward, but was insufficient for attaining, the human end; it bears as well on how the Old Law could and could not be a school of the virtues for the Jews. Thomas contrasts the end of human law ("the temporal tranquility of the community") with that of divine law ("to lead human beings to the end of eternal happiness").[8] Human law is thus content to forbid and punish certain sins, while divine law must make human beings able "to participate in eternal happiness in every way (*totaliter*)."[9] The Old Law resembled human law because, although it forbade sins, it could not confer the grace necessary to fit men and women for this higher end. While good, it was imperfect.

In his reply to the objections Aquinas begins a more complex explanation of how the Old Law, laid upon sinners, served to teach in unexpected ways. The ceremonial precepts (commanding how God was to be worshiped by the Jews) required rituals of purification but did not purify in fact; nonetheless, they required that human beings confess their sin, their need for purification.[10] Thus while inefficacious, the precepts brought to the observant mindfulness of their sin. Thomas turns next to an objection arising from St. Paul's claim that the Old Law "entered in so that sin (*delictum*) might abound" (Romans 5:20). The Old Law is said to have killed (*occidisse*) by providing an opportunity for sin, not by being the cause of sin; the Old Law did this both by making the sin more grave because of explicit prohibition and because it inflamed concupiscence, since forbidden things become more desirable.[11] Thus the Old Law, commanding but not assisting, may have increased sin. Note the possible—and curious—connection between the purpose of the ceremonial precepts and the effect of the Old Law sketched in the second response. The Old Law promoted mindfulness of sin in part by commanding confession of sin and, perhaps, by providing the occasion for it.

In question 98, article 2, Thomas continues his initial discussion of how the Old Law served to teach. Thomas, in arguing for God's authorship of the Old Law, stresses its function as a propaedeutic. The Old Law bore testimony to Christ (by prophecy), and it "drew human beings away from idolatry and confined (concludebat) them to the worship of the one God, by whom humankind was to be saved through Christ."[12] This again seems a fairly straightforward account of the Old Law's incompleteness: it conduced toward God but could not alone cause men and women to achieve God. But Thomas again complicates the account in a reply to an objection.

> God sometimes permits some to fall into sin so that then they may be humbled. Thus did he wish to give a law which human beings by their own powers were unable to fulfill: so that, while relying on themselves, they would discover they were sinners, and, humbled, turn to the help of grace.[13]

Here Thomas states a more subtle pedagogy at work in the imposition of the Old Law. The Old Law did not lead us toward God in any simple, yet incomplete, way; we first, because of sin, needed to learn how far we were from God. We learned, by our inability to keep the Old Law, that we were sinners and required the help of grace.[14] On this view, built into the Old Law itself was a basic impotence. It could not accomplish what it commanded. It placed burdens on the Jews which could not be borne. Thomas's explanation for this: the futility of its commands was part of its pedagogical purpose.

The full significance of our inability to keep the Old Law becomes clearer as Thomas establishes that the moral precepts of the Old Law, those prescribing acts of virtue, belong to the natural law, since they derive from "natural reason."[15] We must learn (or relearn) the natural law because sin obscures our understanding of it and of our end; at the same time, we discover that we cannot do what we know to be good. The work of the Old Law is to teach us the natural law.

In the last article of question 98, Thomas gives a more detailed description of this education in the natural law as he addresses directly the historical appropriateness of the Old Law. Thomas argues that it was "most appropriate" for the Old Law to be given at the time of Moses because of the effects that law has on two sorts of people: those who are "hard and proud"; and the good, who, "having been instructed by the law, are helped to fulfill what they intend."[16] The Old Law dealt differently with the bad and the good, and its success in dealing with them required in part intervention at the proper time.

Therefore it was appropriate that the Old Law was given at such a time for the overcoming (convincendam) of human pride. For man was proud of two things—knowledge and power. [He was proud of] knowledge, as though natural reason were sufficient for salvation; thus, so that his pride should be overcome in this regard, man was given up to the rule of his reason without the support of a written law. And man was able to learn from experience (experimento) through this that he suffered from a defect of reason, since around the time of Abraham human beings fell into idolatry and the basest vices. Therefore it was necessary after this time that a written law be given for the remedy of human ignorance. . . . But after man had been instructed by the Law, his pride was overcome by weakness, since he was not able to fulfill what he knew. . . . With regard to the good, the Law was given as an aid, which indeed was especially necessary for the people since the natural law had begun to be obscured through the profusion (exuberantiam) of sins.[17]

Here we are given a much more detailed narrative of the pedagogy of the Old Law. The Old Law taught not merely by any propositional instruction; it provided a kind of moral education that was an education for and about our nature. It instructed the good by clarification of the natural law, which habitual sin had obscured. The proud it taught by abasement: that they were not sufficient unto themselves. It humbled them by providing, with the clarification of the natural law, the occasion for discovering that still they could not do what they knew to be their good.[18]

Why was this necessary? How exactly did sin impair natural knowledge of the good?

Thomas explicitly states that, after the Fall, knowledge of the natural law was lost gradually and only in certain respects. In question 98, article 6, Thomas provides two reasons why God did not give the Old Law immediately:

> because at that time man, confident in his own reason, did not yet recognize (recognoscebat) that he had need of [the Old Law], and because at that time the direction (dictamen) of the law of nature was not yet obscured by the habit of sinning.[19]

Thomas clearly indicates here the progressive character of human ignorance of the natural law. Later he describes further in what way the long habit of sinning served to cause this ignorance. While the most universal precepts of the natural law could not be forgotten, yet reason was obscured in what to do in particular.[20] What began to be lost was the ability to determine properly, and to apply, the most general precepts of the natural law. But this ability, as I have argued in the last chapter, is precisely the work of prudence. Thus Thomas seems to say that the habit of sin having taken hold, and the moral virtues having eroded, prudence was increasingly lost as well.

In this way Thomas sees the loss of the knowledge of the natural law as a consequence of persistent and ongoing defection from the good. In the previous chapter, I suggested that in Thomas's view we discover the natural law through a process of reflection on the goods of our nature and on what conduces to those goods. This reflection is characterized as a kind of practical reasoning within experience; we reason about our actions and, more comprehensively, our lives as proceeding toward those goods which constitute our flourishing. In doing this, we appropriate more and more the directednesses which are the core of the natural law.[21]

Thomas, in depicting the effects of sin in the community of the Jews, shows us what occurs when human beings do not so appropriate the natural law. The longer and deeper inordinate attachments went, the fainter grew our knowledge of the natural hierarchy of goods to which we were ordered originally. The more we distorted that hierarchy in action, the less we embodied it in our lives. Thus losing the prudential ability to specify and apply the natural law is a symptom of the failure to enact (to possess actively) the natural law.[22] We lose prudence even as we lose the active directedness towards those goods to which the natural law conduces.

Notice that this explanation can also help us make sense of Thomas's earlier remarks regarding the barbarian Germans' ignorance of certain precepts of the natural law. As their customs, i.e., long-standing practices of their community, encouraged robbery of other societies, so too did they lose an awareness of the illicitness of the activity. The natural law was not lost entirely, either by the Jews or by the German robbers or by any other human community after the Fall, a possibility explicitly denied by Aquinas, as we have seen.[23] But the directedness to specific goods that is the primary sense of the natural law is a directedness that must be discovered and enacted through specific choices and reflected in the order of a life. If this does not take place, then the *inclinationes* of the natural law are rendered inefficacious in directing the person to his or her good.

Men and women can appropriate these directednesses in various ways; we may attain flourishing in different communities with different social practices and forms. But any such practice or custom may on no account violate the natural hierarchy of goods. This is the absolute constraint on differing ways of appropriating the natural law: the natural variation in communities in their social life and customs must be in accordance with the value of the goods themselves as they stand in relation to the created order and in relation to God.

The job of the Old Law was to reawaken the Jews to the law of their natures, and the reawakening had to involve a reenactment or repossession of orientation to the good.[24] The first part of this project was to cause them to realize that they had broken that law and could not reform without God's help. It is no accident that Thomas cites idolatry in particular as the vice which characterized the depth of ignorance (of the natural law) to which humanity had sunk; idolatry may be the most extreme perversion of the natural hierarchy of goods (worshiping human artifact as the Godhead). Recognition of this vice thus would constitute the most stinging rebuke to human knowledge and pride.

If practical knowledge of the natural law was lost gradually, so too was it repossessed only gradually and through experience. Thus God gave the Jews a law which was, for sinners, impossible in its stringency. This law placed before their minds not only the good but their own sin as well. In so doing, it at least caused the Jews to withdraw their affections from false or lesser goods and to turn them towards God (even if only in anticipation of satisfaction). In this way, God required them to enact, to reorient themselves to, the natural law as directednesses to a hierarchy of goods.

The Old Law as Pedagogue

Indeed, one can interpret the whole of the Old Law as initiating and structuring the process of reorientation. Not just the moral precepts, but the ceremonial and judicial precepts as well, required the Jews to enact a directedness to God and to finite goods properly ordered in relation to God. For example, Aquinas explores in what ways temporal promises, promises about goods in this life, were employed appropriately by the Old Law. He explains that the Old Law "disposed to Christ as the imperfect to the perfect."[25] The Old Law induced observance of its precepts at first with appeals to temporal goods, which the Jews already desired; it did this with a view to moving the Jews towards the perfection of adhering to "spiritual things" and scorning temporal goods. The temporal promises made by the Old Law were not simply a pandering to cupidity because they were about goods to be enjoyed "in right order (in ordine) to God," and as coming from God.[26] Finite goods can be promised and enjoyed in this age of imperfection, so long as such enjoyment is not taken to constitute the human end itself. Thus the Old Law gradually withdrew the affections of the people from temporal things: by training them away from inordinate attachments to them, towards the ultimate end of inclining them to the love of spiritual things alone.[27] In this way, their affections were shaped to reflect more closely the value of goods as those goods fall in their natural hierarchy ordered to God. This was, at least in part, what it meant to order their lives according to the hierarchy of *inclinationes* which are at core the natural law.

But it was not simply the promises of the Old Law which caused the Jews to enact a new, more appropriate relation to God. All the precepts of the Law—moral, ceremonial, and judicial— can be understood to continue this project for the community of the Jews. In this regard, one can understand the Old Law as a kind of divinely instituted civil law, being law binding on one specific society.[28] One might also be led to think then that it was ultimately an instance of human law, but Aquinas explicitly denies this. Indeed, he draws repeated contrasts between human law and divine law.[29] The ends of the laws are distinct: human law's end is "friendship of men with each other,"[30] and the end of divine law is to "constitute the friendship of man with God."[31] Likewise, both laws determine further the natural law, but the determinations are distinct as well, because the ends towards which the precepts are ordered are distinct. The Law of the Jewish community had as its end the union of its people with God.

The divine law further determines and amplifies the natural law with a view to ordering men and women to God. Thomas tells us that while the moral precepts are of the natural law (to be discussed further below), the ceremonial and judicial precepts are of the divine law insofar as they are further determinations of natural law, distinct from the more general moral precepts themselves.

> Therefore to honor God, because it is an act of virtue, pertains to a moral precept; but the determination of this precept, namely, that God be honored with sacrifices or gifts of such a kind, pertain to the ceremonial precepts.[32]

The ceremonial precepts ordered the people to God by "certain external works, by which man professes his servitude to God (*divinam servitutem*)."[33] The judicial precepts ordered men and women to God as they are "determinations of the justice to be observed among men."[34] Functioning in this way as a kind of communal law ordering the Jews to God, they may then be understood to conduce towards social habits and forms in new consonance with the natural law.[35]

An illustration is in order: In explaining the pedagogical function of the ceremonial precepts, Thomas recurs again to the claim that law is imposed on two sorts of people, those "prone to evil" and those "having an inclination to good."[36] In this way, he links his remarks to his earlier discussion of how the Old Law was appropriately given at the time of Moses, a discussion which employed the same distinction.[37] The ceremonial precepts, which were many, dealt with each sort of person differently.

> For in that people were some prone to idolatry, and for this reason it was necessary that they be called back from idolatrous worship, through the ceremonial precepts, to the worship of God. And because men served idols in many ways, it was necessary, on the other hand, to establish many ways of suppressing each single way [of idol-worship]. Again, [it was necessary] to impose many things on such people, so that as though weighed down by these things, by which they were devoted to the worship of God, they would have no time to serve idols. With regard to those who were inclined to good, the multiplication of the ceremonial precepts was necessary: because through this their minds were referred to God in diverse ways and more constantly, and because the mystery of Christ, which the ceremonial precepts prefigured, brought many benefits (*utilitates*) to the world.[38]

Thus the Old Law sought to rehabilitate the idolatrous, i.e., to instill in them new habits of right worship; it did this in part by constituting many new practices to supplant the old. While the ceremonial precepts could accomplish only an incomplete redirection, since they commanded only external acts, they at least were intended to crowd out acts of idolatrous worship. Those already virtuous benefited from the precepts by an intensification of their attention to God.

For the virtuous and the idolatrous alike, Thomas's interpretation of the purposes of the ceremonial precepts acknowledges the social forms in which the vices or virtues are imbedded. To root out idolatry, God commanded as law for the entire community a new set of precepts determining the right worship of God. The precepts were numerous so that, as comprehensively as possible, members of the community were able to enact, at least in external worship, a new ordering to God. The very number of the precepts also curbed the freedom to pursue the vices of the past. The judicial precepts as well, being determinations of the natural law pertaining to relations between persons, were laws for the regulation of life in a reordered community.[39]

The Decalogue and the Law of Nature

Let us now turn to Aquinas's discussion of the moral precepts of the Old Law. The chief function of the divine law, we have been told, is to "constitute the friendship of man with God," and this requires that men and women become like God, i.e., good.[40] The special function of the moral precepts was to make the members of the community good as a means, at least in part, to friendship with God. Thus the moral precepts commanded "all the acts of the virtues."[41] These precepts commanded acts of intellectual and moral virtue; thus would men and women be well ordered in their reason properly and in relation to "interior passions and external works" as well.[42] The moral precepts conduced in this way towards the acquisition of the virtues, and far more directly than the ceremonial and judicial precepts.

In question 100 of the prima secundae, Thomas begins a more detailed explanation of his earlier claim that the moral precepts were of the natural law. Aquinas argues that all the moral precepts of the Old Law were "of the law of nature."[43] "Those *mores* are called good which are in congruence with reason. . . . [E]very judgment of practical reason proceeds from naturally known first principles, as was said above."[44] The moral precepts are about good *mores* and thus proceed in some way from naturally known

first principles, that is to say, from the most general precepts of
the natural law. From these first principles, however, judgments
follow in different ways depending on what is being judged. Some
matters are clearly and with very little consideration subject to
approval or disapproval "through these general first principles."
Thomas places in this category of judgments precepts from the
Decalogue such as "Honor your father and mother" and "You
shall not kill." Some other matters are judged after "much consideration of diverse circumstances"; only the wise are able to
accomplish this with the proper care. The precepts are learned
by the community through instruction by the wise; Thomas's
example is a precept commanding respect for the aged. Finally,
there are some matters for which human judgment requires "divine instruction, by which we are taught about divine things."
Thomas includes in this group the precepts of the Decalogue
forbidding the making of carved likenesses and forbidding the use
of God's name in oaths. All three kinds of judgments fall under
the natural law, says Thomas, because all three are derived from
natural reason. But the precepts governing each sort of judgment
pertain to the natural law in different ways.[45]

The moral precepts of the Old Law can all be reduced to the
Decalogue, Aquinas goes on to argue.[46] God himself gave the
Decalogue:

> Therefore those precepts belong (*pertinent*) to the Decalogue of
> which man has knowledge from God himself. Of this kind are
> those which can be known at once from the general first principles
> with only a little consideration and again those which become
> known at once from faith infused by God.[47]

These distinctions of course refer back to the three categories of
natural law judgments given in the first article of the question.
Thomas claims that the Decalogue contains the precepts of the
first and third categories, those knowable almost at once because
of their evidentness to reason and those knowable because God
reveals them. The second category, the teachings of the wise,
belong to the Decalogue as more determinate "conclusions" are
contained in their less determinate principles.

Thomas tells us that the moral precepts of the Old Law all pertain to the natural law, but in different ways. These moral precepts are all themselves condensed in the Decalogue; the Decalogue is itself a set of precepts belonging to the natural law. Let us turn to a discussion of the Decalogue's precepts in order to understand why and how the natural law was given again in this form.

Aquinas sides with Augustine in his ordering of the Decalogue. The first three of its precepts are ordered (*in ordine*) to God, to how men and women should conduct themselves towards God; seven are ordered to neighbor and how he or she should be respected.[48] But the precepts are ordered as well according to the kind of action or attitude they prescribe or prohibit. For example, the precept commanding a rejection of false gods ("You will not have strange gods before me") Aquinas understands as including the precept forbidding the making of images. This latter precept was intended, on his view, to apply solely to the worship of images,[49] so that the law combated idolatry among the Jews. Thus this precept attacked by prohibition the same vice which the ceremonial precepts, as we have already seen, sought to exclude by substitution.

The Decalogue appropriately includes precepts regarding only God and neighbor, says Thomas. For it is the purpose of divine law to "order men to a community or republic under God."[50] To this end, it mandated expression of "fidelity, honor, and servitude" to God. It also forbade harm to be done to one's neighbors, "neither in act nor in speech nor in mind." But the Decalogue did not prescribe duties to oneself, Thomas explains, because this was unnecessary. Sin had obscured the natural law concerning what to do with regard to God and one's neighbors, but this obscurity did not extend

> as far as love of oneself, because the natural law was still strong in this regard. Or again, [no precepts were needed] because love of self is included in love of God and neighbor, and a man truly loves himself when he orders himself to God.[51]

Even at this stage of Thomas's treatment of the Decalogue, we can see connections between the function of these moral

precepts and that of ceremonial and judicial precepts. All of
the precepts—ceremonial, judicial, and moral—were directed to
the formation of a community, and of individuals within that
community, properly ordered to God and to created goods The
ceremonial precepts were meant to create new customs of worship
to supplant the old, idolatrous forms. In this way they were
to contribute to a reordering of the community of the Jews to
God, at least by legislating certain acts of reverence for God. The
judicial precepts as well were formulated to secure justice among
persons within this community ordered to God. Now we see
how the moral precepts ordered the Jews to God—by clarifying
for them the very nature of the natural law. The precepts of
the Decalogue specified what a right ordering was to God and
neighbor. Since the Jews mistook their true good, the Decalogue
corrected them: men and women act to achieve their own good
when they order themselves to God. While the ceremonial and
judicial precepts determined certain external actions which were
in keeping with the natural law, the moral precepts did nothing
less than command the ordering to God which is the natural
law itself. The ceremonial precepts were meant to encourage
a reordering of the Jewish people to God and to finite goods
through new practices of worship; the moral precepts specified
in its commands this reordering. The precepts were directed to
the constitution of persons properly ordered to God and to the
other goods of their natures.

This reorientation of the Jews to God and to created goods
is the very reason for the precepts' absolute status, according
to Thomas. None of the Decalogue's precepts are "dispensable,"
i.e., none admit of exception.[52] Dispensations are made to laws,
Thomas tells us, if observance of the letter of the law (*verbum
legis*) would be contrary to the "intention of the legislator." Now
the intention of any legislator is

> ordered principally to the common good and secondly to the
> order of justice and virtue, by which the common good is con-
> tained and itself achieved. If therefore there are precepts which
> themselves contain the preservation of the common good or the
> order of justice and virtue, such precepts contain the intention

of the legislator, and for this reason are indispensable. . . . And the precepts of the Decalogue contain the very intention of the legislator, namely, God: for the precepts of the first table, which are ordered to God, contain the order itself to the common and final good, which is God. And the precepts of the second table contain the order of justice to be observed among men: namely, that no one do what is undue, and that to each should be returned what is owed. for in this manner are the precepts of the Decalogue to be understood. For this reason, the precepts of the Decalogue are altogether indispensable.[53]

Aquinas understands the precepts of the Decalogue, which are of the natural law, to be, in part, articulations of what virtue is as it pertains to God and life in community. (Recall his earlier remarks regarding the natural law and the Old Law containing precepts about acts of all the virtues.)[54] These precepts do not express merely contingent means to the good; they define in part what it is to be just to others and to give God right worship. When observed in the spirit of the divine law or of the natural law properly understood, namely, out of desire for the goods to which the law directs us, these precepts help to specify what virtue is and their observance is constitutive of virtue. For God to dispense someone from these, Thomas says, would be to dispense someone from the very ordering of himself or herself to God.[55]

Thus the moral precepts of the Old Law conduced directly towards the acquisition of the virtues. That is to say, the Decalogue was directed toward constituting men and women who are good and thus capable, by divine similitude, of friendship with God; this friendship, as we know, is the end of the divine law. But in saying that the Old Law conduced and directed towards virtue and to likeness to God is not to say that it achieved this end. Indeed, in subsequent articles of question 100, Thomas reminds us of the limits of the Old Law and of the need for grace. In that regard, he recurs to his earlier theme of the Old Law's basic impotence.

Immediately following his treatment of the indispensable nature of the Decalogue's precepts, Thomas clarifies what the Old Law commanded and what it conduced toward. The "mode of virtue" did not fall under the precept of law, he tells, although it conduced toward it.[56] While the law may have commanded acts of virtue, it did not command that they be done out of a virtuous disposition necessarily.

> [T]he intention of the legislator is twofold: first, that to which the precept is intended to conduce, and this is virtue. The other concerns that about which the precept is proposed; and this is what leads to or disposes to virtue, namely, acts of virtue. For the end of the precept is not the same as that about which the precept is given, just as neither in other things is the end the same as what is [conducive to] the end.[57]

So the moral precepts (and, to a lesser degree, the other precepts) were intended to conduce towards a reordering of the Jewish people to God; the perfection of this state would be the constitution of a virtuous people who would perform the acts the Old Law commanded out of virtue. But the Old Law itself did not specify this virtue under a precept. That is to say, it did not command the acts be done in this mode.

Moreover, Thomas tells us that the Old Law could not in fact bring men and women into friendship with God. It could not by itself accomplish the reordering to God that it intended. The "precept of charity" within the Decalogue—commanding that God be loved with the whole heart—Thomas understands to require that "all things be referred to God."[5] But this is impossible to do without real charity, which is infused only with grace. Lacking the help of grace, those under the Old Law could not entirely fulfill its precepts.[59] Neither could the Old Law "justify" in the sense of conferring true justice, says Thomas, because true justice is also infused only through grace.[60]

Prudence, Community, and History in the Old Law

Let us review Thomas's characterization of the Old Law in order to clarify what the Old Law contributes to an understanding of how we learn the natural law. All the precepts of the Old Law were directed to the reorientation of the Jewish people to God as their end and to finite goods under God. The moral precepts, with the judicial and ceremonial precepts as well, helped the Jews to reclaim the natural law as an active directedness to God and to other lesser, genuine goods of their nature. The moral precepts were ordered to this end by "containing" the intention of God regarding an ordering to the human end and an ordering to justice between members of the community. In this respect, the precepts recapitulated the natural law. The ceremonial and judicial precepts further determined the natural law in a way that was binding for the Jews alone: they determined in what ways God would be worshiped and in what ways justice would be expressed among members of the community. In this way, they are subordinate to, and contingently specifying of, the Decalogue's more general precepts. What Thomas stresses about all the precepts are their basic inadequacy. They could not justify; they could not all be fulfilled without grace. The Old Law was not able efficaciously to order the community of the Jews to God.

Indeed one of the most striking features of the Old Law, and of the natural law reasoning it employed, was the highly contingent and historical nature of its precepts. The ceremonial precepts, further determinations of the natural law regarding worship of God, were intelligible only in the light of the Jews' history of idolatry. The need for correction created by this history, Thomas tells us, explains the number and the expansiveness of the ceremonial precepts. Even the moral precepts, which would seem more likely to be invariant or, after a fashion, "timeless" were contingent in several respects. They prescribed and prohibited only concerning those matters about which the natural law had become obscured because of the effects of sin, i.e., about what was due to God and to other members of the community. In this way, their pedagogical function acknowledged historical need. Likewise, they were also formulated to address, at least in part, the vices which had sprung up within the community. Thus the Decalogue prohibits the making of carved images for worship in order to root out the practice of idolatry. All of this is to say that the Old Law comprised determinations of practical reasoning that are fully intelligible only in the light of the Jewish community's history and circumstances. The Old Law was tailored (by God and by Moses, its mutual givers) to the needs of a specific community at a specific time.

But the community is needed as well for the knowledge of the Old Law in certain respects: certain precepts of the natural law, as contained in the Old Law, can be discovered reliably only by the wise. The wise then instruct others.[61] Thus, even with the special revelation of the Old Law, the exercise of prudence is still needed for determination and application of the natural law. In this sense, the Old Law and human prudence work in tandem to secure the articulation of the natural law to the community.

But prudence is at work not only in this regard. It might seem that the precepts of the Old Law—specific, numerous, and comprehensive as they were—rendered the exercise of prudence unnecessary for those under that law. On the contrary, the Old Law conduced towards an active appropriation of the natural law. Such an appropriation involves growth in a prudential understanding of the human good and how to achieve it; it also involves an affective reorientation to the good. So through the Old Law, the Jews (at least the most virtuous of them) came better to understand and to desire their genuine good; they came, as part of this, to desire more ardently union with the God who gave them the Law.

The distortions and errors of other interpretations regarding the character and function of law for Thomas become increasingly clear. Rather than being obtusely inflexible, as Strauss and Jaffa claim, the natural law is fitted in its articulations to the exigencies of community and history. Some of its determinations by the Old Law were highly contingent and context bound, as in the ceremonial and judicial precepts. Others, while invariant, still admitted of application by prudence. And their invariance sprang from the fact that they helped to constitute the goods to which they ordered the community: without justice to God and others, and without refraining from certain destructive acts, the human good could not be constituted at all.

Since the Old Law's precepts determined or expressed the natural law, we then can also see how the natural law is understood by Thomas to be both discovered and applied in an ongoing historical process. And what do we learn, from the narrative history Thomas provides about the Jewish people, about the natural law?

The natural law, we already know, is the rational creature's possession of eternal law; by the free exercise of reason and will he or she discovers and enacts that law. But after the Fall the rational creature's attempts to keep the natural law, even with the help of the Old Law, led to the discovery of his or her subjection to sin. This discovery, and this subjection, occurred within community and within the developing history of that community. In this respect, I believe the history of the Jews is understood by Thomas to share much in common with other communities wrestling with the long-term effects of sin. Of course they were also special because of their place in salvation history. God chose to give the Old Law not to all, but to some; not to one, but to a community. He did this, Thomas emphatically states, by gratuitous choice, not because by special fidelity the Jews deserved the gift.[62] But in his description of the Jews, Thomas provides one narrative history of a community first forgetting, and then seeking to recover, the natural law. Thus his claims about the Jews' subjection to sin can, I think, be generalized to all communities before the entry of the New Law into history. The German robbers did no better.

As a consequence of sin, what we begin to forget is our true good.[63] To this degree, we forget our own natures and, thus, the natural law; this is why a corrective was needed even before the New Law entered in. The Old Law, by its clarity and authority, defied misunderstanding. Yet even then we discovered that we could not keep it. The Old Law taught us what our good is and taught us that we cannot achieve our good by ourselves. In this regard, the Old Law (or the natural law so appropriated) points beyond itself to the remedy for sin—to the New Law, which is the grace of Christ. The inadequacy of the Old Law and its subordination to the New Law is, like the Old Law itself, something which was possessed and enacted.

Thus all under the Old Law, both the "hard and proud" and the (at least partially) virtuous lived out, in their individual lives and in the life of their community, the essential incompleteness within the Old Law. The proud experienced it, Thomas has suggested, in their continuing and humbling subjection to sin. The virtuous experienced it by a more sustained attention to God, through the Old Law. But bear in mind that even for those who most claimed and enacted the Old Law, it could only promise, but not fulfill. For a very long time, until the coming of Christ, the Old Law could only order men and women, imperfectly, towards God. Possession of God was always beyond reach (a harsh discipline for idolaters).[64] Perhaps this, too, was part of the Old Law's pedagogy, as though God said, "Let them know desire for me, real desire, before they know contentment of that desire." The New Law is the law of love that accomplishes friendship with God.

4. NATURAL LAW AND THE NEW LAW

In turning to the New Law, to the law that enables achievement of God, we must first examine in greater detail how Thomas argues for God as the ultimate human end. This will clarify what the work of the New Law must involve in effecting union with God and will prepare the way for an explanation of how the natural law, which orders men and women towards God, is related to the New Law.[1]

Human Beatitudo

As noted in chapter 2, Thomas begins the secunda pars of the *Summa* with a discussion of the ultimate end of humanity. In doing so, he duplicates Aristotle's strategy in the *Nicomachean Ethics*. In many ways Thomas also follows Aristotle in certain conclusions of his inquiry: all human beings act for an end;[2] there is a final end;[3] the final end is that for the sake of which all else is willed.[4] In specifying the nature of the ultimate human end Aquinas shows how he both accepts Aristotle's conclusions about happiness and yet finds them wanting.

In the last article of question 1 of the prima secundae, Thomas distinguishes between two ways of interpreting the term *end* (*finis*): as that in which the good is found or as the "use and attainment" of that good.[5] Thomas then deploys this distinction to describe how God is the end for creatures.

> Therefore if we speak of the ultimate human end as that thing which is the end, all other things come together [in sharing] in the ultimate human end, because God is the end of man and of

all other things. But if we speak of the ultimate human end as the attainment (*consecutionem*) to the end, in this respect nonrational creatures do not partake of this end. For man and other rational creatures attain (*consequuntur*) their end by knowing and loving God. Other creatures are not capable of this; they attain the ultimate end insofar as they participate in some likeness to God according to which they exist, or live, or even know.[6]

All creation imitates, by "similitude," God's reality insofar as every creature is inclined to the full actualization of its nature. Since God is the author of all good and all actuality, all creatures tend towards God when they tend towards the fulfillment of their own natures.[7] In this way the full actualization of a creature faintly echoes, or distantly resembles, the actuality of God.[8] But rational creatures have the capacity, according to Thomas, for actual attainment of God in knowledge and love. Knowing and loving God implies some measure of possession of God's own self.[9]

Union with God constitutes the human end because no created good, or set of goods, can satisfy fully the human appetite for the true and the good.

> For the object of the will, which is the human appetite, is universal good, just as the object of the intellect is universal truth. From this it is clear that nothing is able to satisfy the human will except universal good. But this is not found in anything created, but in God alone, because all creatures have a participated goodness.[10]

In denying that beatitude can be any created good or state of soul,[11] Thomas quietly subverts Aristotle's own conclusions about the good for human beings. Aquinas rejects the claim that any state of natural human flourishing can appease completely the human desire for good; at the same time, he clearly holds that human *inclinationes* have a connatural end, that is, an end proportionate to human powers of attainment. One could understand Aquinas to sketch the goods constitutive of this end in his description of the "order" of the *inclinationes* in the prima secundae, question 94, article 2. But the connatural end is not our ultimate end. The achievement of our good in strictly natural terms leaves us, according to the structure of our powers of intellect and will, "metaphysically" unsatisfied;[12] beyond this, the happiness accessible to men and women in this life is itself flawed. Asking if happiness is attainable in this life, Thomas denies even the possibility (quoting Job in the sed contra). The vision of God's essence will occur only after death [13]

> For beatitude, which is perfect and sufficient good, excludes every evil and fulfills every desire. In this life we cannot exclude every evil. The present life is subject to many unavoidable evils: ignorance of mind, inordinate desires of the appetite, and many pains within the body. . . . Similarly, the desire for good is not able to be satisfied in this life, for man naturally desires the good he has to be permanent. But the good of this life is transitory; even life itself is transient.[14]

Aquinas expresses the complex unsatisfactoriness of natural happiness; not only does it fail to sate human desire for the good, but it is prone besides to many positive evils external as well as internal to the will (because of the effects of sin). The natural happiness which serves for Aristotle as the human end Aquinas finds wanting, "imperfect." It does not satisfy even Aristotle's own formal requirements for a fit *telos*, on Aquinas's view: it is not complete, not sufficient. Neither is it permanent or invulnerable to disruption, stipulations which are Thomas's own.[15] Thomas does not, however, deny the goodness of natural goods; he simply argues that they cannot constitute the ultimate end for men and women. Indeed, he denies a constitutive place to all goods other than God in the ultimate end. Both friends and external goods are needful for the "imperfect happiness" of which Aristotle speaks, but neither is necessary for union with God which is the whole and perfect happiness of men and women.[16] We are in fact satisfied by God alone; but this ultimate end we cannot apprehend in this life.

The highest knowledge of which human beings are capable naturally is best described as a knowledge of first principles; constrained by the limitations of sense knowledge, we cannot know essentially what is immaterial.[17] In this regard, Thomas argues for the unsatisfactoriness of "speculative science," the fruits

of natural contemplation, as a candidate for the human end:
"Our intellect is reduced to actuality through the consideration
of speculative knowledge, but not to its ultimate and complete
actuality."[18] Any natural knowledge of God stops very far from
the vision of God's essence that Thomas describes as the ultimate
human end, which is beyond our natural powers of attainment.[19]

> All knowledge which is according to the mode of created sub-
> stance falls short of the vision of the divine essence, which exceeds
> infinitely all created substance. So neither man nor any creature
> can arrive at the ultimate end through its own natural abilities.[20]

Yet Thomas does understand the beatific vision to be a kind of
completion, or at least fulfillment of intention, of what is desired
in natural contemplation. Thomas casts the vision of God as what
will bring to an end—by fulfillment—the human desire to know,
which desire initiates philosophical inquiry.[21]

While we cannot achieve God on our own, still our natural
reason can lead us to turn to God—by seeking the assistance of
grace. With God's help, we then are enabled to attain God. In this
respect nature is not lacking in what is necessary, Thomas says,
quoting Aristotle, since, "'what we can do through our friends
we can do in some way through ourselves.'"[22] How we become
friends of God, and thus able to possess God's own self, is the
work of the New Law.

The New Law as Law

Aquinas initiates his discussion of the New Law with questions
bearing upon its status as law. He inquires as to its form, its
scope, its origin, and its end. Calling the lex nova the "law of
the Gospel," Aquinas states that it is "principally the grace of the
Holy Spirit, which is given to believers in Christ."[23] This primary
sense of the New Law is to be distinguished from any secondary
sense involving written precepts and prescriptions. Aquinas goes
on to compare it explicitly to the natural law:

> There are two ways in which a thing can be instilled (inditum)
> into a human being. First, as pertaining to human nature, and

thus the natural law is a law instilled into human beings. In a second way something is instilled as being superadded to nature through the gift of grace. In this way the New Law is instilled into human beings, not only indicating what should be done but also helping to accomplish it.[24]

This point is repeated time and again by Thomas in his treatment of the New Law: it is not a set of laws governing external behavior but instead an internal prompting to God directly. In one sense, it resembles the natural law: both laws are primarily ways of being directed to an end. But while the natural law directs men and women to their natural end, and to God according to their natural capacities, the New Law directs them to union with God as their ultimate and supernatural end. In fact, the New Law enables believers to achieve the highest end: union with God. It is of the nature of the New Law, understood as grace, to justify, says Aquinas; it makes possible the salvation of those who possess it.[25]

The grace of Christ which is the New Law Thomas understands as essentially a "special love, which draws the rational creature above the condition of its nature to a participation in the divine good."[26] The gift of grace is a quality of soul; it provides a kind of supernatural principle of action, enabling the rational creature possessing it to move, and to move "sweetly and promptly," to its supernatural end. God alone is the cause of this gift, Thomas argues; only God can "deify" the creature in making it share in a special way in God's own nature.

> For the gift of grace exceeds every faculty of a created nature, since it is nothing other than a certain participation in the divine nature, which surpasses every other nature. . . . Thus it is necessary that God alone should deify [deificet], communicating fellowship [consortium] with the divine nature through a certain likeness of participation, just as it is impossible that anything other than fire should ignite.[27]

This is how we can achieve our ultimate end—by God conferring upon us a sharing in God's own nature. Such a sharing begins here, in this life, but is completed in the beatific vision.

Grace is itself distinct from the virtues infused with it into the soul. Aquinas argues that grace, which raises humanity to a sharing in God's nature, provides a kind of necessary metaphysical ground, or a kind of elevated nature, for the infused virtues: "[Grace] is not the same as virtue, but it is a certain condition (habitudo) which is presupposed by the infused virtues as their principle and root."[28] We will treat further of the infused virtues, especially the theological virtues, later; let us now flesh out Thomas's account of the New Law.

Thomas has already argued for the primacy of grace in describing the New Law. Any written precepts attached to the New Law are secondary to the grace of the Spirit; they are ordered to the instruction of the faithful as to the "use of this grace."[29] How does the law of the Gospel so instruct? It does not fail to direct external acts, although "the kingdom of God consists principally in interior acts."[30] The New Law thus includes the sacraments, and it can prescribe or prohibit those actions which themselves are essential or inimical to virtue.[31]

The New Law directs far more comprehensively the "interior acts" of men and women; indeed, Christ's words in the Sermon on the Mount "contain a total representation (informationem) of the Christian life."[32] Christ orders us there with regard to our own persons, teaching us to avoid evil in every way, both in external actions and in "interior acts." Likewise, the Sermon directs us as to "the intention to the end," commanding that we not seek "human glory" in the good actions we perform. We are also ordered with respect to our neighbors; we are forbidden to judge any of them unjustly but also are cautioned against "committing holy things to them if they are unworthy." Finally, the Sermon teaches the way to fulfill the doctrina of the Gospel: by asking for God's help, by seeking perfect virtue, and by exercising caution against corrupting influences.

It is important to note Aquinas's manner of treatment of the Sermon on the Mount; he understands these words of Christ to express, in lapidary form, a pattern of the Christian life. Aquinas calls the Sermon on the Mount an informatio, a representation or model, of the Christian life. The Sermon itself is in part maxims and explicit *praecepta*; it is composed perhaps more predominantly of certain encomia (for example, "Blessed are the pure in heart"; "Blessed are the peacemakers") and more metaphorical or figurative lessons ("You are the salt of the earth"; "You are the light of the world"; "Consider the lilies of the field)."[33] Aquinas seeks to draw out the meaning of the lessons in more explicit terms; he understands the Sermon to be showing the way to perfection of life. That is to say, the expression of how to live the Christian life is not primarily or exclusively a list of precepts and prohibitions. Thomas leaves open, as he takes the Gospel to do, the matter of in what forms of life such perfection may be achieved. One may be a peacemaker, pure in heart, the light of the world, and like a lily of the field, in a multiplicity of ways.[34] In this respect, the New Law clearly distinguishes itself from the Old Law, which multiplied precepts and ritual observances, and thereby constituted a highly specific, even regimented, form of life, for the better control of the unruly members of the Jewish community.

The New Law is called the "law of liberty" because the grace of Christ is not constrained to one form of expression; neither is the Law itself, although it demands perfection of act and intention, experienced as oppressive. For, as in the case of even the more explicit precepts of the New Law, the assistance of grace is presupposed for the fulfillment of what is taught by the Gospel. Were this not so, the "law of perfection," requiring perfection in act and intention, requiring comprehensive ordination to God, would only overtask those under it. "For even the letter of the Gospel would kill, unless the healing grace of faith were present within."[35] Without grace, the New Law would be even more burdensome than the Old.[36]

Thomas in fact argues for the historical appropriateness of the New Law precisely in how it completes and achieves what was intended in the Old Law. Thus while the Old Law was "like a pedagogue of children," the New Law is "the law of perfection, since it is the law of charity."[37] While the Old Law enforced obedience by fear and by offer of temporal reward, the New Law gives to men and women the desire to act virtuously for its own sake; thus it is "the law of love." The gift of right desire, what might be called holy desire, is repeatedly stressed by Thomas as the core of the New Law in order to articulate how the New Law relies more heavily upon the goodwill of believers, as opposed to explicit prohibition and prescription, and upon the help of grace.

Still the Old Law played its crucial part in preparing for Christ, according to Thomas. The Old Law was needed to teach men and women their need for the "law of grace" won by Christ's redemption.[38] The pedagogy at work in the Old Law, specifying right worship of the true God and teaching the need for grace, is completed in the New Covenant, which is the very presence of Christ among the people and which gives the grace for which men and women have looked for their healing. What the Old Law promised and signified, the New Law accomplishes. "Thus the New Law is said to be the law of truth, and the Old Law is said to be the law of shadow or figure."[39] Still, Christ fulfills the Old Law and does not destroy it, on Thomas's view; only the ceremonial precepts lose their binding force, in fact become inappropriate, since what they prefigured has come to pass in Christ.[40]

Successor to the Old Law, the New Law will itself know no successor. It will continue until the end of the world, because no other law or direction for human beings is necessary: "for nothing can be nearer to the ultimate end than what immediately brings [human beings] to the ultimate end."[41] The grace of Christ raises men and women to participation in the life of God, who is their ultimate end. By raising men and women to such participation, the New Law accomplishes what the natural law intends—although through a glass darkly—and what the Old Law foreshadowed.

And what is accomplished? Thomas describes in his treatment of the New Law how nature is not only healed of sin but raised up to a new sharing in the life of God. Comparing the New Law to the natural law, Thomas emphasizes that the New Law confers a new relatedness to God, the fruit of which is an ease and joy in doing what is good. This new relatedness, accomplished by the grace of the Spirit, is essentially an orientation to God as God is, just as the natural law is essentially an orientation to our connatural end. The orientation achieved by the New Law thus cannot be aptly represented by any catalogue of acts to be performed or precepts and prohibitions of any kind. Rather than informing a life through a multitude of specific outward observances, the New Law is a way of life marked by the indwelling of grace given varied expression.[42] Just so Thomas takes the Sermon on the Mount as his representation of the Christian life, in which the life of grace is described and exalted in forms requiring interpretation and amplification. That is to say, the appropriate "use" or enactment of grace possessed relies heavily upon the mature judgment of believers

We may still press the issue of how grace so works upon believers. How does grace operate to reorient men and women to God, especially in relation to natural faculties and habits? To address these questions, we must discuss virtues infused with grace into the soul.

Charity and the Life of Grace

Within the prima secundae, Aquinas describes the theological virtues with special emphasis on their relation to the natural, "acquired," virtues. Following Aristotle, Thomas acknowledges virtues which are acquired by habituation and which order us to our connatural end.[43] But on Aquinas's view, such virtues are inadequate for human need because our connatural end is not our ultimate end. Thus there are, infused with the presence of grace into the soul, other virtues which order men and women directly to God. Chief among these are the theological virtues, faith, hope, and charity; these take the name *theological*, Thomas explains, because they are infused by God into the soul (and thus are not acquired by any human exercise), because they direct us to God, and because they are revealed by God in Scripture.[44] God directs us to our connatural end by reason and will, but the natural powers of reason and will are inadequate for ordering to God.

> Hence it was necessary that something be added supernaturally to both [intellect and will] to order [humanity] to its supernatural end And first certain supernatural principles are added to the human intellect, which are held by the divine light; these are what

is to be believed (*credibilia*), about which is faith. Secondly the will is ordered to this end: both in terms of a movement of intention inclining itself to this end as possible to attain, which pertains to hope, and in terms of a certain spiritual union, through which it is transformed in a certain way into that end, which occurs through charity. For the appetite of a thing is moved, and tends towards its connatural end, naturally; this movement results from a certain conformity of the thing to its end.[45]

Thus from the very first Thomas sets up the special primacy of charity among the theological virtues, holding that *caritas* is actual possession of the loved object, while faith and hope imply separation from God.[46] For this reason faith and hope will, in the beatific vision, no longer exist, while charity will be made perfect: "For vision is a certain cause of love . . . and the more perfectly God is known, that much more perfectly is God loved."[47] The work of charity proves essential for the theological virtues to perform their function of ordering men and women directly to God.

Thomas specifies carefully the "order" among the theological virtues. In the order of generation, he tells us, faith and hope are prior to charity· because we must apprehend God (in faith) and incline toward God in whom our good can be found (in hope) before we can love God as good (the love of charity). But in the order of perfection, charity is prior to all. Charity, possessing God, although imperfectly in this life, orders all the other virtues to God directly. No true virtue—that is to say, no virtue conducive to attainment of our ultimate end—exists without charity; in the absence of charity, other virtues could not attain directedness to God as God is.[48] Because charity performs this crucial function, it is called the *form* of the other virtues, being the efficient cause by means of which all other virtues are made virtues. Likewise, Thomas explains, charity is called the root of the virtues: charity provides life to the virtues, referring them to God. And just so it is called the mother of the virtues:

> Charity is said to be the end of the other virtues because it orders all other virtues to its end. And because a mother is she who

conceives in herself, by another, for this reason [charity] is said
to be the mother of the other virtues, because by commanding
them, it conceives the acts of the other virtues by desire for the
ultimate end.[49]

Charity orders to God not only the acquired virtues but faith and
hope as well. Charity animates faith in God, making it perfect
in assent to what is believed; it also justifies hope for happiness
with God, enabling one to hope for God because of the merit
one has through the assistance of charity.[50]

Still we cannot say, essentially, how charity performs its function of so ordering the other virtues to God; Thomas employs
metaphors of connection and dependence ("root"; "mother"). A
precise description of how charity works is not possible because
we cannot say exactly what it means to attain God. And we
cannot know God essentially in this life, even though we may
attain God in charity.[51] Our participation in God's life through
grace, in this life, is not the final vision of God that awaits the
justified. Charity, a virtue of the will, not the intellect, attains
God in love, but this attainment is not knowledge, is not vision.[52]
Yet, as Thomas notes with regard to charity, it is better, in this
life, to love what is higher than humanity than to know it—
because cognition requires that the object known conform itself
to our own epistemic constraints, while love attains to the object
as it itself is.[53] Therefore love is better than cognition of God
in this life, while we are in via, because God is achieved without
alteration of the mode of divine being. Thus although the beatific
vision is characterized as chiefly a cognitive act, charity, a virtue of
the will, is for the wayfarer the form and mother of the virtues.[54]

How then does Thomas characterize the possession of God
in the love which is charity? Drawing on Christ's words from
Saint John's Gospel ("I call you not slaves but my friends"),
Thomas appropriates the Aristotelian notion of friendship to new
purpose.[55]

> Charity signifies not only a love of God, but also a certain friend-
> ship with God; which adds, besides love, a mutual return of love
> for love and a mutual sharing, as is said in the *Ethics* 8. This

pertains to charity, as is clear from what is said in 1 John 4: "He who dwells with charity, dwells with God, and God in him." . . . For this society of man with God, which is a certain familiar conversation [conversatio] with him, is begun in the present through grace and is perfected in the future by glory.[56]

Within his detailed treatment of the theological virtues in the secunda secundae, Thomas carries forward his characterization of charity as friendship. He describes the friendship between God and humanity as involving a kind of "communication" of God's own happiness to us, and he again invokes the image of a "conversation" between God and those who love God.[57] And this intimacy with God confers as well a new wisdom born of connaturality with God.

> Rectitude of judgment can be reached in two ways: in one way by a perfect use of reason or, secondly, through a certain connaturality with those things about which one is judging. Thus, about those things which pertain to chastity, one judges rightly through an inquiry of reason if one has learned moral science, but one who has the habit of chastity judges rightly about these things by a certain connaturality with [chastity]. . . . For this sympathy (compassio) or connaturality with regard to divine things occurs through charity.[58]

A kind of intuitive affinity for God and for what conduces towards God, the connatural wisdom conferred by charity is a wisdom distinct from (but not opposed to) the rational deliberation of prudence. This wisdom from the Spirit is not merely speculative in nature; it uses what it possesses in contemplation for practical guidance.[59]

Just as in his discussion of beatitude, Thomas is, in his description of charity, engaging, and perhaps subverting, Aristotle's ethics.[60] In his description of charity as friendship and as the attainment of God, Aquinas seems to contravene Aristotle's notion of friendship. Aristotle explicitly denies to the affiliation of unequals the title of complete friendship;[61] moreover, philia consists, on his view, more of loving than of being loved, and the best expression of friendship occurs when a friend is loved according to that friend's worth.[62] As such, these pronouncements would seem to prohibit an appropriation of *philia* as a way of describing the relation between God and the people God saves. What relationship could be more unequal? How can men and women love as much or in the same way as the God who loved them even in their sin? But Thomas grounds his appropriation of friendship by his explication of grace and charity. Grace raises us to a new connaturality with God; we are "deified," he has said. Understood in these terms, God creates friends for himself. And we can love God for what God is, according to his "worth," because God has made us able to do so; Thomas describes charity, in distinction from hope, as that (supernatural) virtue which enables us to love God as God is in himself. Aristotle, discussing inequality in friendship, says that we would not wish our friend to become a god, since then the inequality between us would be too great to sustain a friendship.[63] Within the Thomistic understanding of grace, not only are we raised up to share as friends in the life of God, but we wish the same for all (for our friends and enemies alike).[64] In this sense, a new ground is discovered for harmony, for community, as well as for reconciliation, among persons.

Aristotle saw the nearest human approach to the divine to occur within *theoria*, contemplation.[65] This activity was, on his view, solitary and essentially more excellent than other human activities—since by it we become godlike. By adopting the social virtue of friendship as the paradigm for charity, Thomas recasts the most excellent human activity: he holds the love of God in charity to be the activity that both is highest and confers kinship with the divine. Even when this union with God will become fully cognitive in the vision of God awaiting the justified, love of God will only increase and become perfect. Thus all the distinctive aspects of contemplation are achieved within the exercise of a form of friendship; in the beatific vision, we will see God as God is, we will be like God, and we will engage in an "intimate conversation" with God, as friend to friend.[66] In this regard Thomas brings together, in the *telos* of his ethics, the goods of both the human and the divine as Aristotle understood them.[67]

Indeed, the gift of wisdom which springs from a connaturality with God both "contemplates divine things in themselves" and

judges in practical matters according to divine rules or standards
(*regulae*).[68] Thus the contemplative and the practical are not
divorced for Thomas; charity, an intimate friendship with God,
animates practically those possessing it.[69] Following Augustine,
Thomas explains that the seventh beatitude in the Sermon on the
Mount ("Blessed are the peacemakers, for they will be called children of God") corresponds to the gift of wisdom. The structure
of the beatitude is split into two parts: the first phrase describes
the "merit" achieved; the second, the reward conferred.

> Now those are called peacemakers who make peace either in
> themselves or in others. And in either of these cases this is
> achieved by putting in appropriate order those things in which
> peace is constituted. . . . And for this reason peace making is
> appropriately attributed to wisdom. The reward which pertains is
> spoken of: "They will be called children of God." Now those are
> called children of God who participate in the likeness of the only
> begotten natural Son . . . who indeed is begotten wisdom. And
> thus by participating in the gift of wisdom, man attains sonship
> to God.[70]

The wisdom from above makes men and women virtuous and
teachable; it also orders them well with regard to their neighbors,
engendering compassion and good works.[71] Again, the fruit of
this wisdom is a new harmony with others through the trans-
forming power of charity; through it, men and women come to
participate, "connaturally," in the being of God. This participation
of friendship establishes a peace reflected not just within the life
of one justified but in the relation of the justified with others.

Nature and the New Law

What charity accomplishes, then, is the essence of the New Law: it
redirects not only the actions of individuals but their desires, their
motivations, throughout their lives; charity reorders the whole
person, comprehensively, to God. The New Law, also called the
"law of charity," accomplishes in this way kinship with God. In

this regard, the law of charity perfects, but also surpasses, the pedagogy of the Old Law. The Old Law's work was to teach the Jews the natural law; the Old Law helped the people, in their relations with one another and with finite goods of all kinds, to realize and enact a right ordering to God and other goods. But still, under the Old Law, they did not possess God. What grace makes possible through the theological virtues is the formation of a person whose life embodies in a radical way an ordination to, and attainment of, God as ultimate end.[72] This attainment is characterized by Thomas as the love of friends, an "intimate" communication of God's own self to the men and women who are God's friends. Within the life of grace, the lives of believers reflect now not just a right valuation of the natural hierarchy of goods; such lives enact a desire for, and an animating love of, God above all else. This is of course in keeping with the natural law; but the New Law accomplishes, in establishing "connaturality" with God, an end beyond natural powers of attainment or even understanding.

For, as we have noted, the attainment of God in the New Law is only partial—at least for the "wayfarer."[73] There is not in this life apprehension of God's essence. Thus an important problem arises: in practical reasoning, we cannot use as a guide an end which we do not—and cannot—apprehend.[74] What then is the ethical standard to be used by believers within the New Law? While the wisdom which comes with charity gives some practical guidance, nothing indicates that it is intended to replace, or preempt, the work of prudence. Rather, Thomas sets it alongside prudence in his initial discussion, suggesting that both judge rightly, but for different reasons.[75] One can in this respect pose the question thus: What is the relation between the natural law (or the standard of natural reason) and that of our ultimate end? Thomas in fact speaks about the effects of grace in regard to certain judgments of natural reason.

To begin with, Thomas speaks of grace as conferring a new disposition toward finite goods. Infused with the theological virtues, he tells us, are moral virtues, distinct in kind from those acquired by habituation. These infused moral virtues complete the reorientation of the justified towards God through an altered attitude towards material goods.

The theological virtues order us sufficiently to the supernatural end in a beginning way, namely, immediately to God's own self. But it is still necessary that the soul be perfected in ordination to God in regard to other things, through other, infused, virtues.[76]

These new, infused moral virtues dictate a different mean from that of the acquired moral virtues with respect to finite goods. For while the justified cannot apprehend God in this life, still they can love God more and more. And this love can be diminished by attachments to goods which, because of concupiscence, pull the man or woman away from love of God above all else towards an attachment to lesser goods.[77]

In the taking of food, for example, the mean set by human reason is that it should not hurt the health of the body nor impede the activity of reason. But according to the rule (*regulam*) of divine law, it is required that man "castigate his body and compel it into servitude" through abstinence from food and drink and in other ways.[78]

Now ordered to God in grace, the justified adopt (freely) disciplines to draw their affections away from material goods and pleasures. The infused moral virtues thus dictate a more ascetic attitude to the goods of the body, not because the goods of the body are no longer goods, but because of the infirmity of the human will in controlling impulses toward sensuality. Without the infused moral virtues, the souls of the justified would be unable to enact a coherent—and progressive—attainment of God as last end in their lives.[79]

But nowhere does Thomas suggest that the acquired virtues fall, as it were, into disuse, or that they become functionless. He indicates rather that they function alongside the infused moral virtues. The infused moral virtues order humanity to its ultimate end *simpliciter* (simply, without qualification), Thomas says, and thus are "perfect."

And the other virtues, those that are acquired, are accordingly virtues, but not indeed virtues *simpliciter*. For they order man well with respect to the ultimate end in some specific sort [of action], but not with respect to the ultimate end *simpliciter*.[80]

The acquired moral virtues do not effect a connatural union with God, as do the infused virtues, but they are capable of directing men and women in more limited ways. In what ways? Thomas does not offer a developed reply at this point, perhaps because his rhetorical emphasis here is on the ultimate end of union with God. He does distinguish between the work of the infused moral virtues,

> through which men conduct themselves well in ordination to their being "citizens with the saints and members of the household (*domestici*) of God" [Ephesians 2:19] and the other acquired virtues, through which men conduct themselves well in ordination to human matters.[81]

This remark suggests a comparison. The infused moral virtues order men and women to community with God. Perhaps the acquired virtues guide human conduct especially in matters related to the common good in society; they may help to achieve the goods of human community understood in natural terms.

Thomas clarifies the role of the acquired virtues within the life of grace in his treatment of prudence as a cardinal virtue in the secunda secundae. (Thomas counts all the cardinal virtues, including prudence, as moral virtues.)[82] In this discussion, Thomas treats of both acquired and infused prudence. He begins by taking up the proper end of prudence generally. Its end is practical, he argues, the bringing about of the human good.[83] Thomas then goes on to extend the work of prudence beyond attention to the good of one individual, to "the common good of many."[84] Indeed, Thomas says, the good of the individual can only be achieved within the community's good.[85] Prudence exists in different ways in one governing a community and in those who are governed.[86] In this discussion, Thomas is not, however, compelled to distinguish explicitly between the work of acquired and infused prudence; it is in raising the issues of sin and grace that Thomas provides material for such a comparison.

In article 13 of question 47, Thomas takes up the question of whether prudence can exist in sinners. Arguing against this claim, Thomas asserts that only one form of prudence is "true and perfect"

> by which [prudence] takes counsel rightly, judges, and commands with regard to the good end of an entire life. And this alone is said to be prudence *simpliciter*, which cannot be in sinners.[87]

A prudence which discerns means to a bad end is a false prudence, true, but still imperfect, prudence considers only a restricted good end, not "the common end of human life as a whole."[88] Thus perfect prudence, as described here, might be acquired or infused; Thomas does not specify whether the end of human life of which he speaks is supernatural or natural.

In the next article, Thomas takes up whether prudence is present in all who have grace. Here he explicitly distinguishes between the acquired and infused virtue. Infused prudence, he tells us, is infused with charity into the soul.[89] In this sense, all who have grace have prudence, since it is charity that perfects all the virtues. Taking up the issue of whether such prudence confers the necessary industry (*industria*) for "foreseeing well what ought to be done,"[90] Thomas distinguishes between the activities of infused and acquired prudence.

> Industry is twofold. One is in fact sufficient with regard to those things which are necessary for salvation. And such industry is given to all who have grace. . . . The other industry is ampler (*plenior*), through which someone can have foresight (*providere*) for himself and for others not only about those things which are necessary for salvation but even about whatever pertains to human life. And such industry is not in all having grace.[91]

Here again, just as in the prima secundae, Thomas invokes the usefulness of acquired virtue in securing the natural goods of human life. Infused prudence is sufficient for the end of salvation, giving one the discernment to determine (and do) what is necessary to this end.[92] But it does not confer ability and experience for directing matters with regard to this life, even as it is subordinated to God. In referring to the "other industry," presumably industry given through acquired prudence, Thomas suggests a cooperative or collaborative effort between the infused and acquired virtue. He does this by the inclusive way in which he describes the work of acquired prudence in this regard: not only does the person have industry for what is necessary for salvation (this conferred by infused prudence) but he or she also has industry with regard to obtaining the natural human good. Thus the industry arising from acquired prudence supplements infused prudence's industry for salvation with a providence for the goods of human life here and now.

Thomas asks, in the following article, if prudence can be in us by nature; he responds that the most universal principles of action are in us by nature (through *synderesis*), but that "posterior universal principles" are acquired "through discovery according to the way of experience or through teaching." That is, even an understanding of the ends of prudence is enlarged and enriched through reflection and experience. Likewise, with regard to actions conducive toward these ends, such actions are in no way given by nature. Since prudence most properly is concerned with what is in regard to the end (*quae sunt ad finem*), prudence thus cannot be said to be in us by nature.[93] Note that Thomas again does not distinguish between infused and acquired prudence here; he seems to take what he says to be applicable to both. If this is so, then neither the acquired nor the infused virtue require a cognitive grasp of an end higher than natural reason can provide.

Thomas goes on to assign to prudence, in its various species, the work of care for forms of community.[94] Prudence can be regnative (as possessed by a ruler of a kingdom for the common good), political (as possessed by citizens ruled over for the common good), economic (pertaining to the good of a single family or house), or military (as necessary to repel assaults on the common good). The end to which the various forms of prudence refer is described as "the common good" or "living well as a whole";[95] the most frequently cited authority is Aristotle. I want to suggest that the species of prudence described here are natural, i.e., acquired. Each kind of prudence pertains to the achievement of the common good of society through the right judgment and action of those within the community, in their various roles and in diverse contexts—as rulers or citizens, in families, and even through military action.

Recall what Aquinas has said earlier in the *Summa*, that the acquired moral virtues "order man well with respect to the ultimate end in some specific sort [of action], but not with respect to the ultimate end *simpliciter*."[96] Recall as well Thomas's distinction between the infused moral virtues, which enable men and women to conduct themselves as "citizens of the household of God," and the acquired moral virtues, through which they "conduct themselves well in ordination to human matters."[97] Taking now Thomas's treatment of prudence in the secunda secundae, including his discussion of the species of prudence, we might conclude that each sort of prudence, infused and acquired, directs a person to the human end, understood either as supernatural or natural, and to a correspondingly distinct community. Infused prudence, perfected in charity, enables a person to order himself or herself well with regard to what is necessary for union with God; as such, it confers understanding for what is conducive to becoming "citizens of the household of God," and it commands accordingly. Acquired prudence, on the other hand, is directed to achievement of the natural human good; it enables a person to know and choose what is good for the civil community to which the individual belongs (according to his or her role in that community). Both activities are prudential, on Thomas's view, and both are ordered to the achievement of the human good. But acquired prudence is more specialized, being directed to the communal good of men and women in this life; this good is itself subordinated to the good of God as ultimate end. This understanding of prudence is in accord with Thomas's earlier description of the acquired virtues as ordering "man well with respect to the ultimate end in some specific sort [of action]." For acquired prudence, the specific genus of action which is its province is judging and commanding what is conducive to the human good within a communal context.[98]

Thomas nowhere claims that infused prudence requires access to a standard higher than natural reason can provide; indeed, he expressly denies this in his treatment of the gift of the Spirit which corresponds to prudence, the gift of counsel (*consilium*).[99] What counsel provides is a special kind of direction, from the Holy Spirit, for what pertains to salvation The gift of counsel perfects prudence by rendering it open to the movements of the Spirit, who has perfect and complete knowledge, and thus by allaying the anxiety of uncertainty; in this way human reason is perfected with regard to what should be done by being guided by divine reason.[100] Thomas does not say that the Holy Spirit provides *apprehension* of what is above reason; rather, one possessed of counsel is moved by the Spirit "as though having received counsel from God. Just so in human matters those who are not adequate themselves for the inquiry of counsel require counsel from wiser persons."[101]

Natural reason, discovering and applying the natural law through prudence, guides human law in ordering men and women to virtue in community. The natural good of human beings is not neglected within the life of grace, nor do the acquired virtues fall into disuse. Rather, the acquired virtues have a significant, but restricted, place in achieving the human good in natural terms. Thomas invokes the natural law repeatedly as the standard for justice for human law. Indeed, he argues against a human law which aims too high. He takes the province of human law to extend only to the prohibition of certain vices and to the promotion of virtue. The prohibition of all vices by human law would teach, on his view, contempt for the law by the impossibility of adhering to it.[102] While such a standard of perfection was suitable for the Old Law, because it directed men and women to God, it would be inappropriate for civil law per se. Thus natural reason and natural virtue cannot direct human beings to their last end, within the community of the saints. It is the divine law, especially the New Law, which achieves this through the connaturality with God which grace confers.

Yet the New Law does not fail to apply in matters of human society; rather, it lays emphasis on the root cause of disturbance among individuals in community. Bear in mind that Thomas, following Augustine, describes peacemaking as the work of the wisdom given in charity. Thomas in fact includes peace among the interior effects of charity: joy, peace, and mercy; and he names as sins specifically opposed to peace vices which divide and cause conflict within community. Just as the peace of charity results from the union of all in love for God, so discord and contention occur in the opposition of one human will to another, against the divine good.[103] And deeds opposed to peace are those destructive of community itself: schism, unjust war, and sedition.[104] So the work of the New Law, as carried out by charity in its transformation of the lives of the justified, buttresses the coherence and unity of human communities. But it does this by the transformation of lives, not by the legislation of deeds. In this respect, good human law, as guided by the natural law and as administered by prudence, works together with the New Law.

Within this radical ordering of men and women to God in charity, the natural order of love is not vitiated. The obligations of charity do not violate a natural order of love among persons in this life. When treating of the "order" of charity, Thomas in fact takes pains to show that charity follows natural reason in acknowledging a hierarchy of obligations and attachments. Far from voiding the natural love and debt one bears to parents, to neighbor, to children, charity commands (and accomplishes) a highly specific order of valuation and even intensity of affection. First, God must be loved above all things, then other things through God, beginning with oneself. Love of self (expressed as union with God) takes precedence even over love of neighbor; thus sin cannot be incurred even to save another from sin. Thomas specifically argues against an understanding of charity which involves equal affection for all. While we are bound to goodwill for all (wishing them union with God), we owe more in action to some rather than others. Just so, charity produces greater intensity of emotion towards these some rather than towards others.

For the affection of charity, which is the inclination of grace, is no less orderly than the natural appetite, which is the inclination of nature. for each inclination proceeds from the divine wisdom.[105]

The order of love, both natural and in charity, will persist even in our "homeland" (*patria*), heaven: "nature is not destroyed in glory, but perfected."[106]

For the very notion Aquinas takes up to explain charity as love for God—friendship—has its first application, with respect to us, as a love that obtains between human beings, in natural terms. Thomas uses the notion of friendship in ways Aristotle could hardly have anticipated, but its explanatory power is drawn from our acquaintance with it as a natural bond between persons. Aquinas's repeated invocation of Aristotle's *Ethics* and his appropriation of scriptural references, in his description of charity, stress experiences intelligible through natural friendship: our friendship with God will be marked by a mutual love, mutual association, a communication or "conversation" with one another, and a mutual knowledge. Just so are our friendships with men and women marked. Of course, in this life the knowledge we have of God is only from the articles of faith, to which we assent as believers, or from the knowledge by likeness within the connaturality which grace bestows.

But one might push this point one step further. I spoke in an earlier chapter about the gradual appropriation of the natural law; I argued that we learn about the goods to which we are directed, and of the means to those goods, through practical reasoning engaged in experience. Perhaps, too, men and women grow in the love of God, and in an understanding of what God is, by an acquaintance with other friends of God. If the attainment of God in charity, and charity's ordination of the other virtues to God, is ultimately mysterious, it does not have to be utterly so. We appropriate, and learn to enact, the New Law in part by the influence and example of others engaged in the same project. Of course the basis of the New Law is the grace of Christ, as given by the Spirit; but we learn more about the right use of grace, according to Thomas, through Scripture and through the instruction, implicit and explicit, of others.[107] If the New Law relies for its implementation on the mature judgment of believers, that mature judgment must be developed and then deployed. Here, too, is a place for the work of reason, aided by the infused virtues.

The New Law in this way seems to work in large part with natural reason; what the New Law contributes uniquely to morality is a new characterization of morality's end: intimate union with God.[108] Towards this end the theological virtues, with the infused moral virtues, direct and unify the actions, motives, the whole life, of the believer to God. Thus the difference between the mean set by the acquired moral virtues and that set by the infused moral virtues (regarding the enjoyment of material goods or pleasures) may be explained as the elimination or reduction of distraction from lesser goods in the love for the unseen God. The life of grace gives to friends of God a structuring unity of desire and a consequent peace.[109]

> For the true good is had in two ways, perfect and imperfect, so true peace is twofold. There is perfect peace, which consists in the perfect enjoyment (fruitione) of the highest good in which all desires are united and brought to rest in one object. And this is the ultimate end of the rational creature. . . . The other peace is imperfect, which is had in this world. Because although the principal motion of the soul is at rest in God, still there are certain contrary things (repugnantia) inside and outside [the soul] which disturb this peace.[110]

A man or woman, loving only God as ultimate end, experiences peace in this unification and satisfaction of desire in heaven;[111] this peace is present incompletely in this life. I believe that the higher mean of the infused moral virtues is best understood as an attempt to screen out "disturbances" in the soul's attention to God. In doing so, the love of God is enhanced; charity is increased.[112] Understood in this way, the higher mean of the infused moral virtues does not betoken any grasp of a *telos* higher than reason can provide, but, rather, natural reason operates, in the service of charity, to discipline and harmonize the desires of the justified.

The unification of desire, which is an interior effect of charity, does not entail the neglect of other goods or other persons. Thomas indicates carefully that the order of charity does not disrupt a natural order of love. Further, he acknowledges certain exterior effects of charity: doing good to others, almsgiving, and fraternal correction.[113] But undergirding these effects is the love which is the principal act of charity. This love is directed to God most immediately, but others are loved through God in charity. Loving God as intimate friend and ultimate end does not preclude loving others as fellow participants in the life of God. Thomas argues that this kind of love for others will not fail even in heaven, where "the whole life of the blessed consists in the ordination of the mind to God."[114] While in this life, a person must attend to those most immediately connected with him or her and is then forced to neglect others, however much their need or desert. Such limits will be surmounted in heaven.

> However it will be attained in *patria* that someone connected with one will be loved in many ways. For the causes of worthy love will not remain inactive in the soul of the blessed person.[115]

No longer subject to the limits of material capacity and time, the blessed are not confined in their attention to those closest to them; they may love according to both personal connection and each soul's nearness to God.

Community and the Virtues

The New Law makes possible for men and women the attainment of their ultimate end, an end they could not have achieved on their own. In trying to follow the natural law, the Jewish people (as representative and example of other communities after the Fall) were led to discover their own servitude to sin; the Old Law helped to reorient them to the hierarchy of natural goods in keeping with the natural law. The Old Law did this in part by the multiplication of precepts ordered to the constitution of a specific way of life that was itself ordered to the formation of virtuous persons. But the Old Law could not cause the men and women striving to obey it to achieve God. It could not bestow grace.

The grace of Christ, given by the Holy Spirit, is at the core of the New Law. The New Law, like the natural law, specifically expresses a directedness to an end; the New Law directs men and women, with increasing intensification, immediately to God. Grace gives to human beings a special connaturality with God, making them newly capable of union with God in the beatific vision. In this life, *in via*, we are united to God in love. Charity, the preeminent virtue infused by God with grace, enables the justified to attain God because it enables them to love God as God is. The love which links God with those who love him Thomas describes as a kind of friendship, a form of fellowship, in which God engages with those who love God in a "familiar conversation." In the beatific vision, apprehension of God will be possible, and love will be perfected in knowledge.

But in this life, believers still live out the story of redemption, as portrayed in Scripture, incompletely. Loving God in charity but not yet perfectly united to God, men and women strive both to increase their love for God and to express that love in the world. For Aquinas, love of God and of neighbor is nurtured, and enhanced, by communal supports; Thomas, as we have noted, recognizes how human communities, governed by civil law, can foster and teach pursuit of the good. Beyond these, with greater specificity and comprehensiveness of moral teaching, is the community of believers which is the Church. The community of those still *in via* is linked for Thomas with those who have completed their journey and who now stand before the face of God. Even within the community of believers still on the way, other sorts of society may be freely chosen as a means towards progress in the virtues.

The secunda pars of the *Summa* treats of the end of human beings and how they attain that end: through the instruction of law, of various kinds, and aided by the virtues. In the secunda secundae, following his exposition of the theological and the cardinal virtues (in that order), Thomas concludes with a discussion of particular gifts and states of life; he repeatedly addresses the question of how to realize "perfection." In concluding the secunda pars in this way, Thomas suggests that the virtues can best be realized within specific ways of life, internal to the community of believers, which develop and sustain them. The choice of a particular state of life, such as the religious life, in no way renounces the mature judgment, and the freedom, granted by the law of the Gospel. Rather, such choices may be understood as ways to develop, and then to express, that mature judgment in concrete forms within a life. For Thomas, the rule of life adopted freely by certain believers, to follow the commandments and to practice the evangelical counsels (poverty, chastity, and obedience), is an expression of love both for God and for men and women.[116] Such a rule of life is adopted formally, with a vow of commitment, says Aquinas, also as an expression of love, as a promise to persist, through time, in the giving of one's entire life to God.[117] And by no accident is perfection of life sought most often in community; communities instruct by explicit teaching and by example.[118] The New Law is realized, and appropriated, in the free adoption of membership in such societies. For Thomas, friendship with God may best be achieved with the help, example, and instruction of God's friends in this life. From such friends, from their witness and their influence, believers can learn better what the life of grace requires—and what it promises.

5. PRACTICAL REASONING, TRAGEDY, AND THE LIMITS OF THE NATURAL LAW

It is time now to say more about the notions of narrative and practical reasoning in Thomistic ethics as interpreted in the preceding chapters. The historical and social features of Thomas's ethics that are examined here also lead back to Martha Nussbaum's concerns regarding the possible presence of tragic conflict in the world and how best to characterize the nature of such tragedy.

Perhaps the best place to begin is to say what I am not arguing for as operative in Aquinas's ethics. I am not suggesting that Thomas holds a developed position regarding the narrative nature of experience as it has been discussed in recent philosophical debate.[1] Much of this interdisciplinary debate is phenomenological in method, and it addresses such issues as the nature of temporality and the problem of personal identity or coherence. One is hard put to find material in Aquinas to echo any specific contemporary view advocating the "realism" or "continuity" of narrative in relation to the world. His method of argument and his metaphysical presuppositions do not force upon him many of the questions which occupy philosophers and literary theorists in recent debate. Nonetheless, I assert that Thomas, in perhaps a naive way, presupposes an understanding of temporality and a model of practical reasoning which lend themselves to support of the position that narrative explanation provides the most accurate means of representing and rendering understandable human action and history.

Thomas's comments in the *Summa theologiae* on temporality in terms of human experience are scattered and, of course, not phenomenological in any extended sense. That is to say, Thomas is not engaged in describing the structures of human consciousness, nor is he attempting to represent the felt experience of persons within time. When he speaks of time-experience at all, the feature of it he stresses most is succession (of moments); by this he seems to mean that our experience of time is of a now that is fluid and moving past us. This temporal experience of finite creatures follows from their essential mutability; the eternity of God follows from God's immutability.[2] To admit of temporal experience is to admit of movement and change: "For . . . the apprehension of time in us is caused by our apprehension of the flux of now itself."[3] God, on the other side, is described as seeing all things as now, as a whole.

But Thomas's emphasis on the phenomenon of succession in our experience of time does not imply that time is some artifice of the finite mind imposing order on chaos. Nor is time clearly only an appearance. For Thomas, finitude is real, as are finite creatures. Our experience of time is also real, bound up with the mutability in us and in the world.[4] The proper "measure" (mensura) of mutable beings is time, says Thomas; "according as any being recedes from permanence of being and is subject to change, just so does it recede from eternity and is subject to time."[5]

Thus the notion of narrative as a way of describing human experience, in terms of the perception of succession or sequence in time, is by no means alien to what Thomas himself says about time. But I mean something more by narrative than this very thin claim of sequentiality, which is hardly narrative. When I speak of the narrative nature of our knowledge of the natural law in Thomas, I mean, first, that the natural law (as both knowledge of human nature and what conduces to the flourishing of human nature) is discovered progressively over time and through a process of reasoning engaged with the material of experience. Such reasoning is carried on by individuals and has a history within the life of communities. We learn the natural law, not by deduction, but by reflection upon our own and our predecessors' desires, choices, mistakes, and successes.

Such discovery is not unguided or unconstrained, nor is it entered upon ex nihilo. We have, to begin with, the directedness of our own natures as guide and authority. And human beings are, as part of their natures, social. Each individual is shaped (for good or ill) by his or her civil community's customs, beliefs, and laws, which in turn reveal that society's current apprehensions of what the good is for humanity, and of what is deemed conducive to that good. That is, a society's customs, beliefs, and laws reveal its understanding of the natural law. The development of that understanding is narrative in admitting of certain sorts of real beginnings and ends, as well as of more partial kinds of closure.

An illustration is in order:

Consider Goerner's "case study" of the Germans and how they might be represented as coming to understand the natural law more fully.[6] Goerner claims that the Germans discovered the natural law by incurring the (undesirable) consequences of breaking it. Raiding their neighbors to the point of material depletion, the robbers were then forced to turn to another way of life to feed themselves. According to Goerner, this encounter with the long-term consequences of their practice of raiding taught them, now more fully, the natural law. On my view, Goerner inadequately represents what sort of reasoning must be involved in discovering the natural law as law. To find oneself or one's community in violation of law, and thus to identify undesirable consequences as penalties, requires access to some standard of justice which Goerner does not grant to the Germans; he calls his interpretation the "bad man's view" of Thomistic natural right. He denies to them possession of prudence.

What would argue, in Goerner's description of the Germans, against an interpretation of the Germans' development that belied any moral education and spoke instead of sheer expediency? Such an interpretation might run like this: "The German robbers raided other communities until these communities' resources were depleted. The robbers were then forced to seek out new means to sustain the life of their own society—through constituting a more stable community much like the ones which they had previously looted. But their earlier, more fortunate, way of life they did not forget and recalled with nostalgia." On this understanding, a decision to alter the social practice of raiding would be a judgment of mere expediency. The robbers would reject robbing

because of its contingent unworkableness, not because of any ethical appraisal of their earlier actions. Indeed, this being so, what
would prevent such raiding communities, should their neighbors
become prosperous again, from taking up raiding afresh? This
would be a perfectly rational response: leave off robbery until
there are better pickings. Crime might still pay; just give it time.
All of this is to say that Goerner's reading of the Germans'
deliberations about consequences does not prevent the characterization of their reform as base expediency rather than growth in
virtue. Such reform could not then be characterized as discovery
of the natural law.

Let me put my question about the adequacy of this account in
a more technical way: What is necessary in order to view the consequence of an action as a penalty or punishment for the action?
The interpretation of penalty can only apply if the action is seen
as the violation of a law of some kind; only consequences that are
attached to an action because the action is unjust or in violation
of a law can be intelligibly characterized as punishments. Where
no knowledge of a standard of justice or law exists (independent
of the perception of mere consequence), the concept of penalty
necessarily lacks application.

In fact, Thomas makes clear much earlier in the prima secundae that the evaluation of any action as bad means that one grasps
that the action has fallen short in some way of its appropriate
good. Evil is for him a privation of good; it occurs when a creature
or creature's action is somehow lacking in the good which it ought
to have.[7] To evaluate an action as bad implies, then, that one sees
that it falls short, or causes the agent to fall short, of a relevant
good. But Goerner's account does not allow for this apprehension
of the good by the German robbers; they therefore cannot reason
to the fact that their robbery is evil, according to Thomistic lights.
As I read Aquinas, to attach to an action unpleasant (and very
eventual) consequences, such as material poverty, is not sufficient
to discover that the action is evil.

Aquinas holds that any knowledge of the natural law must
be derived in part from desire for the goods to which men and
women are directed by their natures; this form of directedness is

in fact the primary sense of natural law for Aquinas. This means that people judge what is, or is not, in accordance with the natural law in part by deciding which actions are, or are not, conducive to those goods they so desire. Thus for the Germans to have grasped the fact that the depletion of their neighbors' wealth, and their own resultant poverty, were punishments for violation of the natural law, they would first have had to understand that robbery deprived them of certain goods necessary for their flourishing. Such understanding might well be the product of discovery: of learning about what is truly good for them and of what is not conducive to that good. Such discovery would have to be bound up with reflection upon the various desires they have and with judgment about which desires direct them to their true good. This sort of reflection and decision occurs in part through experience (one's own or another's) with the consequences of choices (one's own or another's).

Perhaps it would be helpful to distinguish at this point between two sorts of consequences and what can be learned from them. The first sort of consequence I call *external*; this may attach to an act contingently or necessarily, but it does not imply the moral evil or good of the antecedent event. This is how I understand Goerner's portrayal of the German robbers' education of the natural law: that the consequences he represents as teaching the Germans the natural law are in fact only external consequences. The most such consequences would secure is the avoidance (perhaps only temporary) of robbery; it would teach only that such action brings unpleasant consequences in the long run. But it would not by itself have taught the Germans that robbery was wrong. To learn that they would have to have had access to a standard of law and a knowledge of the good that Goerner denies to them. Goerner's natural law may curb the unjust behavior; it will not supply the reason for why it is unjust.[8]

But Thomistic natural law recognizes and requires another sort of consequence, one which I will term *privative*. This result attaches to an act necessarily, insofar as the act necessarily deprives the agent (or community) of some good to which he or she is directed by the teleology of human nature. For the Germans to see their robbery as bad, they must recognize that it deprives them of a genuine good; for them to view it as unjust, they must understand that it falls short of what justice should be.[9]

Aquinas defines the cardinal virtue of justice as "a habit according to which someone gives to each what is due him by a constant and perpetual will."[10] Justice is concerned with relations with others and with what, in matters of external property, belongs to others. It is natural for human beings to own property insofar as God gave men and women "dominion" over creation for their use. They require external goods in a certain measure to sustain life, and ownership is a means to this good.[11] The specific rules governing property holding, however, are a rational addition to the natural law, originating in "human consent, which pertains to positive law."[12] But these laws are morally binding, since they serve to preserve the peace in communities and, when broken, can harm individuals as well as the coherence of the society as a whole.[13] This being so, theft and robbery are evil acts, since they involve taking from another, by stealth or by violence, what is rightfully that other's.[14] We may then ask: What did the Germans learn about their practice of raiding so as to identify it as unjust?

At the very least, for learning of the natural law to occur, the Germans must discover that their raiding issues in privative consequences, that is, in results which deprive them of some good or set of goods which they require for their flourishing. They find that their practice of raiding deprives them of the enjoyment of life in stable community and of the goods (and virtues) which such a life would foster. This might, as I have suggested, very well involve discovering that they desire such goods; such discovery could occur within the very experience of finding themselves hungry, their "host" communities picked bare, and themselves forced to take up a more self-sustaining way of life. But still, to decide that the earlier way of life was unjust, was wrong, must involve identifying that law of their natures which directs them towards goods of which their earlier life deprived them, and must then involve identifying to themselves that the consequences of breaking this law were in essence penalties.

Such a history of discovery of that part of the natural law might run thus: "And so, driven by their hunger, the Germans were forced to take up a more stable and agrarian way of life. Over time, after chafing under the burdens of this change, the Germans grew to new understanding. They came to prize the hard-won fruits of their work and the virtues which were necessary to this work. In all this, they found new respect for the communities whose way of life they now shared. They acknowledged that their earlier raiding of these communities had been wrong; it had as well resulted in a dependence that eventually left them without resources."[15] In reevaluating their former social practice, the Germans can then acknowledge the painful external consequences of their hunger and poverty. But they must also come to know that the raiding was unjust: damaging to their own community and to the communities and individuals they robbed.

Such reasoning (and learning) requires the presence of a human nature ordered to a good or set of goods; this is the only way to make sense of the claim that the Germans, by raiding, deprived themselves of their own good. The core sense of natural law is, as I have argued, exactly this for Aquinas: a kind of teleology in human nature possessed within the *inclinationes*. This teleology is mirrored, as well as implemented, in the teleology of action for Aquinas; all action is ordered to an end, and the will chooses always under the aspect of good. The concept of good, under which the will chooses, is given content and further specification through the *inclinationes* directing us to our connatural good. We learn practically, in the desiring and choosing of actual goods, what "good" is and what goods are constitutive of our flourishing. So, I have argued, do *synderesis* and the *inclinationes* together constitute the natural law. But this law must be learned in order to be efficacious as practical guidance, and such learning requires experience over time. We must discover what our good is and what is conducive to that good. In this way, we both understand and enact the natural law. It is of the essence of this kind of teleology, both of action and of nature, to be expressed by development, appropriation, even maturation. Such processes inherently order a creature, in the present, towards the future:

another way to express the necessarily inherent narrative structure
of acquisition of the natural law.[16]

The gradual and developing appropriation of the natural law is
required by the teleology of our natures. The question becomes,
in practical reasoning, what choices to make in order to appropriate and enact our directedness to specific goods. This involves, in
action, seeking to discover what choices will, as Ralph McInerny
has put it, truly "save the formality of the good" under which
we choose.[17] That is to say, we must seek to make those choices
which will be productive of the genuine good for us.

About choices mistakes can be made, and part of the rationality of our choices, and our lives, must involve the process
of clarification regarding what our true good is. Perhaps only
by the living out of our plans and intentions can we come to
understand what we were seeking within those very plans and
intentions. As Abigail Rosenthal puts it, "At minimum, a story
is a purpose transformed into enough experience to allow that
purpose to understand itself a little better."[18] This helps us to
see why discovery of the natural law must be time bound. In the
pursuit (and, often, possession) of goods we learn about what we
wished to attain or should have desired. This is of course a kind
of self-discovery.

The only way to make sense of such a process of discovery as
the German robbers are posited to have enacted is as a kind of
story, or, better, history. Such a history involves some stance of
inquiry on the part of the person(s) in question as well as the
time and relevant kinds of experience to bring that inquiry to
fruition. In particular, practical reasoning such as the Germans
might have performed cannot be purely formal or deductive
in structure. It cannot be formal because there must be some
ordination to the good already present in order to make the kind
of discovery I have described. This ordination must be in some
ways enacted and appropriated, by the (at least partial) practice of
the virtues within experience. To identify certain consequences as
penalties entails access to some standard of justice. Likewise, this
practical reasoning cannot be deductive because it is, as Thomas
notes, a feature of human knowing that we learn bit by bit, by

"acquisition and discovery";[19] we do not know enough, at the "outset" (whatever that could mean), simply to deduce what we should do to obtain our good.

While we do implement certain first principles in action, we return to them, dialectically, to revise and/or enrich these principles in the light of our experience.[20] Life may be an education in what we should do to get what we want; but this education may be about more than instruction in the better choice of the means to the ends that we deemed, originally, worthy of pursuit. We are also taught, through experience, about what our ends ought to be; this education can occur in the very getting of what we thought we wanted. That is to say, it may only be by the making of mistakes that we learn what is and is not conducive to our genuine good, to what truly "saves the formality of the good." This kind of learning is part of what goes on in appropriation of the natural law. Witness the Germans or, for that matter, the Jewish community, who "learned by experience," Thomas says, that their reason was insufficient for obtaining their good.[21] Such a process of learning from mistakes must involve the corrigibility of one's goals and of the (implicit or explicit) goals of one's community. By *goals*, I mean the values, activities, and even possessions deemed worthy of pursuit in action; such goals are inculcated in part by the beliefs, customs, and laws of a community. Thus they reflect in what way the community grasps, or has failed to grasp, the natural law.

Beyond talk about the teleology of nature and the development of our knowledge of the natural law, one further use of narrative operates in Aquinas's ethics. Human history is for Thomas most fully and truthfully explained within the context of the specific narrative of Scripture. Both the Germans and the Jewish community before Christ are explained by Thomas in the context of the Fall, the effects of sin, and the need to return to God through the help of grace won by Christ. Thomas notes that it took time for human communities to lose, after the Fall, their active apprehension of the natural law. When they did lose it, Thomas says it was because of the "exuberance of sin" and the moral distortions caused by it.[22] The rediscovery of the natural law required of the Jews was necessary because of the historical and social loss of the law, caused by an increasing defection from the good. Men and women, after the Fall, gradually forgot the natural law in certain respects; they forgot it as they ceased to enact it, ceased to appropriate it in action.

One might put it this way: the narrative of Scripture contains for Thomas a history of what happens to human beings when they (try to) thwart the teleology of their own natures.[23] Sin, while an offense against God, is also an injury to the creature sinning. And relearning the natural law requires, Thomas indicates in his explanation of the Old Law and the Jews, coming to terms with the authority of this teleology in achieving one's good and the good of one's community. This meant in part, after the Fall, acknowledging one's inability to do the good one knows; acknowledging one's sinfulness, one then must have recourse to the help of God in revelation and grace. The Jews were taught, Thomas narrates, their own insufficiency and need for God by their inability to keep the natural law. In this regard, the natural law has for Thomas an inescapable theological dimension. We are ordered to union with God, but we cannot attain God, even according to our natural capacities, without divine assistance. The Fall, one episode in human history, thus affects in lasting terms the character of human progress towards the good; on Thomas's view, the ongoing human complicity in sin must be acknowledged before men and women can accurately understand (or correct) how they stand in the moral life.

This process of practical discovery of the natural law and of our inability to keep it admits, then, of certain episodes or stages, admits of partial kinds of closure. Scripture provides a history of our possession of God in Eden, of the Fall through sin, of the deepening effects of sin, and of humankind's return to God through reappropriation of the natural law and through the connaturality of grace. Each of these "chapters" of human history can be set off from one another; Thomas treats of the distinct "stages" of this union, fall, and return within the Summa, not programmatically but in terms of the lived narrative of Scripture.

Indeed, the very structure of the secunda pars of the *Summa* can be explained as a partial replication of the Scriptural narrative. A number of exegetes have noted how the questions on law in the secunda pars appear between the thematic treatments of sin and grace.[24] Aquinas's positioning of the questions on law indicates, it is argued, how law is intended as a corrective for sin but is a partial corrective; grace is needed to heal nature and to effect union with God. The movement of the scriptural story is indeed reproduced in the *Summa*'s movement from sin to law to grace. But of course the discussion of law, admitting of various kinds of law, provides also in itself a way of speaking of sin as well as a way of speaking of grace. Thomas treats in passing of the *lex fomitis*, the law of concupiscence which holds sway over human beings since the Fall. Moreover, the eternal law itself, Thomas's core and most comprehensive sense of law, and the natural law which is the rational creature's participation in eternal law, provide a way of describing what the Fall and the ongoing defection from God in sin is a defection *from*. Finally, the New Law is itself the expression that Aquinas adopts for the period of human history marked by the entry of grace; the law of love confers connaturality with God. All of this is to say that the questions of the secunda pars treating of law are linked, in their own internal configuration of topics, to the overall dialectical structure of the *Summa*'s treatment of human beings and their relation to God. Thus it is true as far as it goes, but still too simple, to describe with complete adequacy the placement of the section on law in the prima secundae in terms of the need for law as partial, though ultimately inadequate, remedy for sin Thomas's discussion of law comprehends far more than this insight.

Indeed, Alasdair MacIntyre has read the whole of the prima secundae as a kind of "theoretical recapitulation" of the kind of practical reasoning an individual must perform in order to make progress in the moral life.[25] One would move from the question of what one's good is to how to obtain that good by means of right action and right training of the passions; one could not answer these questions without a knowledge of the natural law and, as part of this, without knowledge that we cannot keep the natural law without grace.[26]

This explanation renders intelligible the structure of the prima secundae in many ways, and it offers a formal, programmatic exposition of the sort of practical reasoning operative in Thomas's ethics. We do not quarrel with its insight into the prima secundae's ordering, although each thematic set of questions in the prima secundae admits, in its own internal structure, of greater complexity than is expressed by a general explanation. The treatment of law is one illustration of this point. But even as a model of practical reasoning for Thomas, this "recapitulation" may be misleading. Thomas's account, as represented in discussion of the Germans and the Jews, emphasizes the necessary communal aspects of inquiry into the good for human beings. Indeed, the whole thrust of his discussion of law, of especially the natural, Old, and New laws, is towards the social—and historical— experience of sin, of gradual reappropriation of the natural law, and of grace. For Thomas, it would seem, practical reasoning by individuals is subsumed under, and profoundly influenced by, the understandings of the good instantiated within specific societies.

Moreover, our account of practical reasoning in Thomas's ethics lays stress on the need for experience and for revision. Appropriation of the natural law requires lived experience over time; it involves the playing-out of present understandings of the good, for confirmation or disconfirmation in experience.[27] As part of this, mistakes can play their part in the discovery of the natural law on either the individual or the communal level, or both. These mistakes can be about what the human good is, in some constituent part of it, or about the proper means for achieving this good. Indeed, in human history after the Fall, it would be surprising if distortions about the nature of our good did not occur in certain areas: because of the (increasing) failure of human beings to enact the natural law. Thomas's own account of human knowledge of the natural law in fact repeatedly indicates that such knowledge is linked to the law's enactment. That is to say, knowledge of the law of nature can be obscured, as he notes, by viciousness of custom or habit, whether in societies or in individuals.[28] Recovery of knowledge requires, then, reappropriation of the law; this would involve first the acknowledgment of error or sin. MacIntyre's theoretical recapitulation, as theoretical, may minimize the degree to which effective practical reasoning in Thomas requires the active assistance of the virtues and the time and experience for discovery in reasoning.

But MacIntyre himself provides what may be a more imaginatively satisfying model for describing practical reasoning of the sort sketched above. In his own discussion of narrative in *After Virtue*, he notes that the narrative stories of our individual lives share at least two common features: they are teleological, i.e., they aim at an end or goal; and they are unpredictable, i.e., they are subject to chance and to the intervention of others. MacIntyre goes on to claim that the moral life is essentially a quest searching for what the good is for us, both as individuals and as members of humanity. He rightly notes: "A quest is always an education both as to the character of that which is sought and in self-knowledge."[29] Such an inquiry is lived out; it cannot be an armchair adventure. For this reason MacIntyre gives the virtues such emphasis: they enable us to live out our questions well, to make progress in our quest. For reasoning well about our good (or discovering the natural law, on my understanding of Aquinas) as a quest is not a process that goes on in a vacuum. We do this work in the midst of, and about, the projects, encounters, relationships, and choices that shape our lives. In this regard, such a quest can be a taxing, trying affair. Given this, we can say Martha Nussbaum has been right to stress the need for courage and for tolerance of ambiguity in the moral life.

I apply this notion of quest to Aquinas's view of practical reasoning; MacIntyre of course makes no such application.[30] Still, such a model can serve as a helpful corrective to the legalistic and aridly theoretical interpretations of Thomas's ethics which have prevailed in the past.[31] In adopting the model of a quest to describe moral inquiry within a life, MacIntyre captures some of the same features of practical reasoning upon which I have focused.

This model's application to Aquinas's view of moral reasoning has limits, however. To begin with, the inquiry or quest into the human good requires, on Thomas's view, the ordination, and then appropriation, of a natural teleology. MacIntyre explicitly rejects Aristotle's (and I assume Aquinas's) "metaphysical biology" in *After Virtue*.[32] Secondly, the inescapable social, and even political, dimensions of knowledge of the natural law do not find pride of place in such a model, as they do in Aquinas's own discussion. Still, what is evoked by the notion of quest is the practical and temporal character of this sort of inquiry. On Thomas's view, efficacious moral knowledge is acquired in part through experience and reflection on experience but is guided by authorities secular and religious.

Tragedy and the Limits of the Natural Law

In treating of Thomas's understanding of narrative and practical reasoning, we need to take up one final concern: the issue of tragedy and the role of finite goods in Aquinas's ethics. Let us recall the key features of Martha Nussbaum's criticisms of Aquinas on this issue and of her own interpretation of tragedy.

To begin with, Nussbaum holds that any type of system which enjoins obedience to a set of exceptionless rules is necessarily inferior to an ethic whose standard is practical wisdom. What practical wisdom can attend to, and what rule following cannot, are all the relevant moral particulars in a situation. Indeed, in an important sense "deductivists," Nussbaum believes, do not correctly see persons and goods as distinct, as independent, and most especially as heterogeneous. This is one fundamental presupposition underlying Nussbaum's case against deductivism: she takes the world to be one in which conflicting claims are made upon the prudent, clear-sighted, moral agent by various goods and persons. The world is "tangled" in its very nature,[33] and to attempt to untangle the demands it makes upon one is to falsify it.[34] Deductivists and other rule-oriented ethicists attempt to resolve tragic conflicts arising out of this tangled world by thus falsifying or eliminating one set of the competing claims.

What does Nussbaum mean when she asserts the "heterogeneity" of objects and persons in the world? What she seems concerned to combat is any system of ethical reasoning which "subordinat[es] the particular claim of each commitment and love to the claims of harmony."[35] Not only does such a system produce, against its own will, as it were, harm through its blindness to others, but it is also

> morally objectionable in that it commits the holder to a systematic neglect of certain features of persons—namely, both their separateness and their qualitative uniqueness—on which their specific personal value might be thought to rest.[36]

Perhaps for these same reasons Nussbaum likewise asserts the incommensurability of goods and persons: as unique, nonrepeatable, and autonomous, they should not be judged or compared within a single system of value. Again, this would result in distortion and neglect regarding the particularity and distinctness of the specific objects and persons under scrutiny.[37]

Thus for Nussbaum, tragic conflict is bound up with the nature of the world: we cannot hope to meet "with perfect fidelity" all obligations laid upon us in the course of our lives.[38] Rather, ethical maturity consists in part of accepting the uneliminable moral conflicts in the world and in responding to them with attentiveness and emotional courage.

I wish to discuss two features of Nussbaum's claims with reference to Aquinas: the issue of the heterogeneity of goods and persons in the world and, as product of such heterogeneity, the issue of tragic conflict. By his natural law reasoning, is Aquinas guilty of the distortions of deductivism? Also, does he in any way acknowledge the reality of tragedy within the world?

To begin with the latter question: Aquinas, in the *Summa*, makes mention several times of something like moral conflict. For example, in the secunda secundae, when treating of justice as a cardinal virtue, Thomas takes up the issue of restitution for past injustice, asking if it is necessary for salvation.[39] In his second objection, Thomas argues that restitution cannot be necessary, offering the example of one who robs another of his or her good name through telling the truth. Since restitution could be achieved in this circumstance only through lying, if restitution were necessary for salvation the "defamer" would be *perplexus*, in a moral dilemma: bound to lie to achieve salvation but also bound to avoid sin. Aquinas, in answering this objection, rejects the possibility that this is genuine, insoluble perplexity. If the truthful defamer makes the truth known (regarding the party in question) in a way that preserves the appropriate order (perhaps in a legal proceeding), restitution is not required at all. While harm has been done to the reputation of the person in question, no injustice has been committed. But if a defamer defames by lying, or even makes the truth known gratuitously, i.e., without due cause, restitution is required because injustice has been done.[40] Note that Aquinas is concerned primarily with moral guilt or innocence here, not with the emotions of the person defaming (or the one being defamed). Thomas does not, however, preclude regret or, for that matter, compassion for the party suffering harm to his or her reputation. He simply rejects characterizing the giving of such injury (when called for) as wrong, as unjust.

Indeed, Aquinas takes up a number of such instances of *prima facie* conflict in the *Summa theologiae*, some of which he dismisses, as in the case of the defamer, as inauthentic perplexity, and others of which involve, on his view, some prior culpable act, error, or omission by the person caught *perplexus*.[41] That is to say, Thomas attempts to resolve *prima facie* moral conflicts by dismissing the dilemma as ingenuine or by assigning fault to the moral agent in question for a sin or error of judgment issuing in the conflict. Thus moral perplexity *simpliciter*, turns out, in the cases he examines, never to materialize: every conflict is either resolvable or (could have been) avoidable. Note that in this way, nothing persuasive, as a defense against Nussbaum's claims, can come of a more detailed exegesis of Thomas on tragic conflict. For she rejects precisely what Aquinas assumes: that beliefs admit of truth-claims and that instances of conflict can then be examined, possibly resolved, by the falsification of one of the conflicting ethical demands.[42]

Indeed, given that Nussbaum claims that tragic conflicts arise contingently, out of a combination of any number of particular concerns and circumstances, it seems unlikely that any *a priori*, "knockdown" argument could be devised against a position such as hers. But Aquinas does not so much as attempt such a refutation of tragic conflict per se; he simply examines possible instances, case by case, and finds a way to resolve them. Still, he keeps generating such cases within his own treatment of specific topics, acknowledging that at least *prima facie* conflicts do occur. Thomas's comprehensive attitude to such conflict seems to be that perplexity *simpliciter* would be unfitting, *inconveniens*; to find oneself, in all innocence, in a situation in which one cannot help but do wrong flies in the face of the providence of God, which is unfailing, on Thomas's view.[43] For this reason, I think Aquinas is disposed to think that perplexity *simpliciter* cannot occur, and he carefully resolves each particular *prima facie* conflict. But in his resolutions, Thomas is concerned with moral culpability, not, as Nussbaum is, with doing justice to the felt experience of the agent in such a dilemma.[44]

Thus Thomas and Nussbaum seem to be working at cross purposes on the issue of moral conflict; they are in many ways working at different projects, with different suppositions, with regard to the same issue. Far more enlightening, and far more fundamental, is their disagreement on the "tangled" nature of the world. For Nussbaum, persons and goods in the world are at root heterogeneous and incommensurable. For Thomas, a mark of the prudent person, one who both enacts and understands the natural law, is that he or she evaluates finite goods according to a single hierarchical scale of value, with all such goods subordinated to God. Is this not still the spirit of deductivism? From the perspective of Nussbaum, Thomas's position might well seem austere, otherworldly, even hostile to the world. Nussbaum's own position, expressing the preciousness, uniqueness, and irreplaceability of persons and goods, seems attentive to what we honor and love in the world. How are we to understand Thomas on this issue?

At the very least, the rhetoric, if not the attitude, of *contemptus mundi* colors Thomas's remarks on the right relation to material goods and to other persons. Short shrift seems to be given to the value of created goods as opposed to God. But what Thomas may have in mind is that too often such goods are indeed opposed to God; Thomas's own rhetoric may be intended to clarify the natural hierarchy of goods, not so as to disdain the created order, but to exalt God as its author and source. The world, to Aquinas, is a created world, and all things derive their being and goodness from God. Just so, the concupiscence to which men and women are prone after the Fall prompts neglect of God for the more immediately gratifying goods created by God. What Thomas suggests in his interpretation of the natural law is that attachment to such goods, without the anchor of a right relation to God, becomes itself distorting and inappropriate. In such inordinate attachments, we lose active knowledge of our own good; we lose the knowledge of how to value other goods as well. Thus while the world may be tangled according to Nussbaum, for Aquinas, it is our desires and loves which can become tangled and at war with one another in sin. The world itself embodies a natural hierarchy of goods which should be, for Aquinas, mirrored in our desires. Recall the effect of peace which is the unification of desire caused by charity. Loving God alone as one's end creates this peace, but loving God does not entail loss of love for finite goods and persons. Indeed, Thomas's discussion of the duties of charity indicates that only when a person embodies a right relation to God is such a person able to know how to love another. To will another's good, on Thomas's view, is to will his or her own union with God. Thus I read Thomas, in his hierarchy of value, not as deriding the goods and persons created by God; rather, Thomas indicates that he is mindful of the ways in which human beings can distort their relationships with what (and who) they love. But this danger is not in the world; it is in ourselves. Nussbaum, on the Thomistic view, mistakes the contingent conflicts bred by our sinful condition for the necessary structure of the world.[45]

Still, let us pursue further this question of tragedy. Is there any notion of tragedy accommodated within Thomas's ethics? Tragic conflict *simpliciter* Thomas is disposed to reject; heterogeneity in the value of goods in the world he also rejects. But it may still be appropriate to locate within his ethics some sense of the tragic in several respects.

To begin with, Aquinas presents the human journey to God as ongoing and historical. On both the individual and communal levels, human progress in pursuing the good requires time, the relevant kinds of experience, and the support of others serving as teachers and friends. The Germans' discovery of that part of the natural law that forbids robbery was historical, occurring over generations, and only with the spur of new experience: would the Germans have learned what they did had they not been reduced to hunger, for example? There thus opens a terrible contingency in our appropriation of the natural law: discovery of our good requires the assistance of conditions quite beyond our control. Should time be sufficiently limited, or experience impoverished, could a community make progress in knowledge of their good? Or correct the knowledge already possessed? With this contingency comes the possibility of failure in discovery.

One can also locate this contingency in the social nature of human inquiry about our good. We are dependent upon community and law to articulate better the natural law for individuals. The Germans are a model of what can go wrong when a whole society mistakes some portion of the natural law. Family, teachers, and friends also function in important ways, even within communities with greater clarity about the good, to educate individuals in the moral life. Community, family, and friends are not influences subject simply to choice by an individual. Here again a kind of "moral luck" is needed.[46] Without right influence and teaching from these sources, is an individual capable, on his or her own, of making effective moral progress? It is certainly true that one's relationships to such influences is "dialectical"; while our choices cannot govern these matters entirely, still our choices can reject, renew, or alter these relationships. In most circumstances, this is sufficient to secure a measure of right influence and teaching, from some quarter. But perhaps not in all cases.

Thus in several ways we may locate a contingency present in Thomas's account of what is necessary to learn the natural law; within this contingency, tragedy emerges as the possibility of a certain kind of privation. Privation of time and experience, privation of proper communal teaching and supports, when profound enough, may damage an individual's (or a whole society's) progress in understanding the human good. Such privations can retard or even, in some cases, prevent appropriation of the natural law. If Thomas should argue that such a circumstance, of one bereft of right teaching and influence to the point of disorientation, is *inconveniens*, and a denial of God's providence, one can only reply that providence is then not always evident in the world. If the guidance of the natural law has a final limit, then it might look something like this· the encounter with epistemic obstacles to its appropriation and enactment so great as to render it impotent. Such a privation might well be deemed tragic in proportion.

Even on the level of the New Law, at least a certain tension between the natural and the supernatural ends of humanity can be uncovered. Recall that grace enables us to attain union with God, a union which in this life is affective only, through the virtue of charity. Recall as well that we have an active directedness to certain connatural goods, within the natural law. Many religious disciplines, of which Thomas speaks, involve the "mortification" of our appetites for material goods in order better to control the waywardness of the will. But, for example, in the instance of martyrdom, the good of life itself is forfeited as a witness to "the truth of faith."[47] Such an act is, Thomas says, "of the greatest perfection,"[48] since it requires the loss of the most primordial natural good as an expression of adherence to the faith. For the sake of the unseen God, the martyr forfeits the life he or she possesses now. To be sure, the intentional sacrifice of a lesser good for a greater would not be deemed tragic by Aquinas; still the immediacy of what is forfeited, and the intangibility of God in the present life, produce a kind of epistemic tension in the choice. The choice thus requires, and manifests, on Thomas's view, the theological virtues at work. Martyrdom, he says, is "a sign of the greatest charity."[49]

But a certain aspect of the martyr's situation, loss of a good already possessed for one yet to be attained (fully), is shared in different circumstances by others within the life of grace. For all, the loss of natural goods, including persons, comes eventually. This involves much of the same "remorse," grief, and pain which Nussbaum deemed appropriate responses to the loss of persons and goods (through tragic conflict). While not active and deliberate forfeiture, the loss of goods and persons still presents a further need for the theological virtues for believers: to remain faithful to the God as yet unseen, even in the light of the loss, with all subsequent anxiety and perplexity, of what we know and love here. For Aquinas, believers live out *in via* the story of the Gospel incompletely; the unassailability of the happiness to be found in union with God does not render our present happiness any less fragile. Or any less dear.

The commonplace of the Christian spiritual tradition that the impermanence and fragility of natural goods constitutes a kind of pedagogy, teaching adherence to the eternal God, may not be the only lesson to be learned; loving God as last end need not entail a diminution of our love for goods and persons in this life. Indeed, it is from friendship in this life that Thomas draws his model for describing the union with God in charity; it is also from God's friends, who are also ours, that we receive instruction here in the life of grace. Thus the New Law may in fact bestow new significance upon the natural goods we love, and their perishability does not detract from their importance. In so loving natural goods, in their mortality and in their dignity, there also is a need and a place for the exercise of the virtues.

NOTES

1. Questions and Concerns

1. Thomas Aquinas, *Summa theologiae*, section 1 of part 2, question 91, article 2, body. Hereafter, the *Summa* will be cited as *ST*, and references will note its particular section and part (1a; 1a2ae, 2a2ae; 3a), question (q.), article (a.), and part of article. Parts of an article are indicated by obj. (*obiectio*, objection—preliminary argument—usually numbered), sed contra (*sed contra*, counterargument), resp. (*responsio*, response—or body of argument), ad 1, ad 2, etc. (replies to preliminary arguments as numbered).

The Latin text is the edition of the *Summa* made by the Institute of Medieval Studies of Ottawa (Ottawa, 1941–1945). Translations are my own unless otherwise noted. In preparing my translations I have studied and consulted the English translation of the *Summa* by the Fathers of the English Dominican Province (*Summa theologica of Saint Thomas Aquinas*, 5 vols. [New York: Benziger Brothers, 1947; reprint, Westminster, Md.: Christian Classics, 1981]).

References to other works of Aquinas will be made in full.

2. *ST* 1a2ae, q. 90, a. 1, resp.

3. Among those philosophers and theologians writing on Aquinas, their engagement with certain central philosophical problems dictates my choice of conversation partners. That is, rather than being driven by the ebbs and flows of current (or past) academic debate, my principle of selection for secondary work to be addressed is thematic and philosophical. Further, my selection of interlocutors is not comprehensive; there are of course other significant exegetes of Aquinas than those I take up substantively or in notes. Some are referred to in the bibliography, below. Two very recent books worth mentioning here are: *Natural Law Theory: Contemporary Essays*, ed. Robert P. George (Oxford: Clarendon Press, 1992); and Ralph

McInerny, *Aquinas on Human Action: A Theory of Practice* (Washington, D.C.: Catholic University of America Press, 1992).

4. Leo Strauss, *Natural Right and History* (Chicago: University of Chicago Press, 1950), 163.

5. Ibid., 164.

6. Harry V. Jaffa, *Thomism and Aristotelianism* (Chicago: University of Chicago Press, 1952), 167–70; see especially 169 for the crux of this argument.

7. Ibid., 183.

8. Martha Craven Nussbaum, "Practical Syllogisms and Practical Science," in *Aristotle's "De Motu Animalium,"* trans. with commentary and interpretive essays (Princeton: Princeton University Press, 1978).

9. Ibid., 168–69. To push her claims about Aquinas, she invokes Maritain and his analogy of human beings as pianos to be tuned to the one true pitch.

10. Ibid., 167.

11. Ibid.

12. Ibid.

13. Martha Craven Nussbaum, "The Discernment of Perception: An Aristotelian Conception of Private and Public Rationality," in *Proceedings of the Boston Area Colloquium in Ancient Philosophy*, ed. J. Cleary (New York: University Press of America, 1985), 151–201.

14. Nussbaum, "Practical Syllogisms," 165.

15. Ibid.

16. Martha Craven Nussbaum, *The Fragility of Goodness: Luck and Ethics in Greek Tragedy and Philosophy* (Cambridge: Cambridge University Press, 1986), 93–94

17. See ibid., especially ch. 4–7.

18. Martha Craven Nussbaum, "Flawed Crystals: James's *The Golden Bowl* and Literature as Moral Philosophy," *New Literary History* 15 (Autumn 1983): 25–50.

19. Ibid., 25.

20. Ibid., 30.

21. Ibid., 33.

22. Maggie, to become practically wise and a mature moral agent, must then accept and grapple with the consequences of her own fanciful ethical system. She must win her husband back· Amerigo has since engaged in an infidelity of another kind with her father's wife, her own best friend, Charlotte. To win him back, Maggie must work harm against her own friend and, in the end, part from her

father forever. Thus repairing the damage caused by her misguided attempts to preserve her innocence and perfection intact leads her, Nussbaum suggests, towards a deeper loss of that innocence than would have occurred originally. Maggie must, in a very deliberate way, "sacrifice moral purity" ("Crystals," 34). It is important for Nussbaum that the emotions accompanying this sacrifice, "among them shame, jealousy, tenderness, respect" (35), are inseparable from the practical wisdom which has taught her to pay attention to the claims of particular persons and relations: "the value of persons and of objects is partially constituted by the risk they bring of pain and opposition" (35). For Nussbaum, this complexity of the conjunction of emotions is the counterpart to the complexities of description which distinguish one situation from another. Both types of complexity individuate and particularize circumstances and events.

23. Nussbaum, "Discernment," 151–201. In "Discernment," Nussbaum gives three reasons why practical wisdom is preferable as a standard to any kind of deductivism. As she puts it, "it is not just that ethics has not yet attained the precision of science; it should not even try for such precision" (175). The deductivist's goal of composing a system of rules to govern every possible situation is a wrong-headed distraction from the proper concerns of ethics; further, as she goes on to argue, it is a delusion, an impossibility as well.

Nussbaum draws her arguments for the superiority of practical wisdom from Aristotle, *Nicomachean Ethics* 1103b34–1104a10, where Aristotle discusses the degree of precision appropriate to ethics and to ethical judgments. First, interpreting Aristotle, she asserts that because "practical matters are mutable, or lacking in fixity," ("Discernment," 175), it is impossible in principle for any set of rules to anticipate what virtuous action must be in every circumstance. Indeed, the virtues themselves are "defined with reference to contingent circumstances that may themselves undergo change" (175); thus the virtues themselves, dependent upon circumstances, are "evolving" and "situation-relative," as Nussbaum reads Aristotle. Given this, she argues that what is needed is not a list of precepts but the good agent's ability to "improvise," given new situations, out of the experience gained in the past; this will involve activity of imagination and emotional response, both of which will emerge out of the good character of the agent. Secondly, the practical has, perhaps because of its mutability, an "indeterminate or indefinable character" (*to aoriston*) (176); this trait is connected with "complexity and context"

(177). Choice must take into account all the features of the given situation in constituting the good, and all this cannot be captured in rules, which are general. The third characteristic of the practical which evades formulation in rules is the presence, in certain cases, of "ultimately particular and non-repeatable elements" (177). Not only can the complexity of a conjunction of facts be unique, unrepeatable; there can also be particular facts that are themselves unique, unrepeatable. Here again Nussbaum wants to champion the moral relevance of particulars over and against any type-differentiating manner of evaluating situations or actions. Further, she seems to equate such type differences with the recognition of only impersonal goods; thus she speaks, in championing the personal, of the relevance of "shared history" between two people and the status of family relationship. Extending this, she suggests that Aristotle views the recognition of uniqueness itself as especially important. One must treat a friend, for example, "as a unique, non-replaceable human being, a being not like anyone else in the world" (178).

24. Nussbaum, "Discernment," 179.

25. Ibid.

26. Ibid., 199.

27. E. A. Goerner, "On Thomistic Natural Law: The Bad Man's View of Thomistic Natural Right," *Political Theory* 7 (1979): 101–22; and idem, "Thomistic Natural Right: The Good Man's View of Thomistic Natural Law," *Political Theory* 11 (1983): 393–418. My summary discussion here is clarified and expanded in my essay "Goerner on Thomistic Natural Law," in *Political Theory* 18, no. 4 (November 1990): 638–49. For a reply to some of my criticisms, see Goerner's "Response to Hall," *Political Theory* 18, no. 4 (November 1990): 650–55.

28. Goerner, "On Thomistic Natural Law," 102.

29. See *ST* 1a2ae, prologue. Goerner discusses this in "On Thomistic Natural Law," 108.

30. Goerner, "On Thomistic Natural Law," 109.

31. Ibid., 111.

32. Ibid.

33. It is termed thus in Goerner, "Thomistic Natural Right," 398.

34. *ST* 1a2ae, q. 94, a. 4, resp.

35. Goerner's discussion can be found in "On Thomistic Natural Law," 114–19.

36. Ibid., 117.

37. Goerner, "Thomistic Natural Right."

38. *ST* 2a2ae, q. 120. Goerner discusses this in "Thomistic Natural Right," 400–412.

39. Goerner, "Thomistic Natural Right," 410–11.

40. Goerner argues that the Germans only took robbing to be acceptable outside of their own community. This was the case, he explains, because "a society that thought all robbery was good would be a society with no stable property . . . [and would possess] . . . scarcely any technical mastery of nature" ("On Thomistic Natural Law," 114–15). This mastery is in some degree necessary for the satisfaction of basic human needs.

41. Goerner, "On Thomistic Natural Law," 115.

42. Ibid., 116.

43. Ibid., 115.

44. This passage and the argument summarized here appear in more detailed form in my article "Goerner on Thomistic Natural Law."

45. See Germain Grisez, "The First Principle of Practical Reason," in *Aquinas: A Collection of Critical Essays*, ed. Anthony Kenny (Garden City, N.Y.: Doubleday, 1969), 340–82, for an example of his early exegesis of Thomas. John Finnis states his version of natural law in *Natural Law and Natural Rights* (Oxford: Clarendon Press, 1980). There is a useful summary of their more contemporary stand on natural law in John Finnis, Germain Grisez, and Joseph Boyle, "Practical Principles, Moral Truth, and Ultimate Ends," *American Journal of Jurisprudence* (1987): 99–151, where they indicate how their own view is no longer intended as exegesis of any other ethical theory (see 100–102).

46. See Finnis, Grisez, and Boyle, "Practical Principles," 101.

47. Ibid., 102.

48. *ST* 1a2ae, q. 94, a. 2, resp.

49. Finnis, Grisez, and Boyle, "Practical Principles," 120.

50. See ibid., 107–8.

51. Ibid., 137–38.

52. See, for example, Germain Grisez's *Christian Moral Principles*, vol. 1 of *The Way of the Lord Jesus* (San Francisco: Franciscan Herald Press, 1983), 184 ff., for a useful discussion of these issues.

53. Finnis, Grisez, and Boyle, "Practical Principles," 110.

54. F. Russell Hittinger is in my opinion the most thorough and persuasive critic of the Finnis/Grisez position. See *A Critique of the New Natural Law Theory* (Notre Dame, Ind.: University of Notre Dame Press, 1987).

55. In fact, Finnis and Grisez explicitly deny that God can be the human end; see Finnis, Grisez, and Boyle, "Practical Principles," 133–35.

56. See, for example, *ST* 1a2ae, q. 91, a. 2, resp. and ad 2.

57. John Finnis, in his recent *Moral Absolutes: Tradition, Revision, and Truth* (Washington, D.C.: Catholic University of America Press: 1991), does make some mention of the virtue of prudence *per se.* He is concerned to defend the existence of "moral absolutes," understanding by that term exceptionless "norms" (3) prohibiting certain sorts of actions and protecting the basic goods of human life. He in particular emphasizes that the prudent person's character will be formed around "*all* the moral absolutes" (83). Such persons will "exclud[e] from deliberation all options which involve the violations of specific moral norms and are therefore unjust or unchaste or in other ways disrespectful of basic human good(s) immediately at stake in possible options" (104–5). But on the traditional understanding of prudence, including Thomas's, the prudent person's character is formed around the moral virtues, habits which themselves exclude certain sorts of actions from deliberation. It would be more helpful for Finnis to provide an account of what the work of prudence should be, within his ethics, rather than what choices it eliminates from consideration.

58. Daniel Mark Nelson, *The Priority of Prudence: Virtue and Natural Law in Thomas Aquinas and the Implications for Modern Ethics* (University Park, Pa.: Pennsylvania State University Press, 1992).

59. Ibid., xi.

60. For a critique of various interpretations of Thomistic natural law, see ibid., ch. 1, 1–26.

61. Ibid., 11.

62. Ibid., 2.

63. I argue for this at length in ch. 2, below; see *ST* 1a2ae, q. 91, a. 2 and q. 94, a. 2.

64. See, for example, Thomas's discussion of prudence as reasoning about the human end, at *ST* 2a2ae, q. 47, a. 2, resp. and ad 1.

65. Nelson, *Priority*, 33.

66. See my discussion of the last end and the theological virtues in ch. 4, below. As I will discuss there, Jean Porter also argues for this position in her work on Aquinas's ethics.

67. Nelson, *Priority*, 113.

68. Ibid., 145.

69. As part of his mistaking the substance of the natural law, Nelson often treats of it only in terms of _synderesis_, the habit by which the first and most general formulation of the natural law is possessed (see _Priority_, 99–100). He treats of _ST_ 1a2ae, q. 94, a. 2, where Thomas discusses the _inclinationes_, in these terms: as Thomas's "merely restating in slightly more detail his claim that the law of our nature is always to act for the sake of an apprehended good" (119). On my view, this is a serious misreading. While Thomas does hold that the will always chooses under the aspect of the good, and while it is true that it is not determined to the choice of any finite good (as Nelson notes, 45–49), the indeterminacy of the will does _not_ vitiate the teleology of our natures, a teleology which is sketched in _ST_ 1a2ae, q. 94, a. 2. The first principle of practical reason held by _synderesis_ is by no means the whole of the natural law.

Nelson makes the mystifying claim that, for Aristotle, prudence "operates without first principles" (144). But for Aristotle, as for Aquinas, the fullest articulation of the first principle will be an account of the end at which we aim. (See Nancy Sherman's excellent discussion of this point in Aristotle in _The Fabric of Character: Aristotle's Theory of Virtue_ [Oxford: Clarendon Press, 1989], 89 and 194–97.) I will offer an account of the natural law in which the _inclinationes_ of the natural law, deliberated on by prudence, give content and specification to _synderesis_ so as to provide such a fuller notion of the natural human end.

70. Nelson is right to note that human law requires prudence (110–11), however, Thomas also states that human law is derived from the natural law (_ST_ 1a2ae, q. 95, a. 2).

71. Nelson does note that development of prudential knowledge of our good is historical and communal (see _Priority_, 151–53), but he does not trace out this insight in Aquinas's thought.

2. Natural Law as Law

1. See Alasdair MacIntyre's discussion of this point and of the structure of the _Summa theologiae_ in _Whose Justice? Which Rationality?_ (Notre Dame, Ind.: University of Notre Dame Press, 1988), ch. 10, especially 170–73. My own thinking here has been generously informed by MacIntyre's discussion of Aquinas and the exercise of

practical rationality in knowing the natural law (*Whose Justice?* ch. 10 and 11).

2. *ST* 1a, q. 22, a. 1. An earlier version of portions of this chapter appears in my "Towards a Narrative Understanding of Thomistic Natural Law," *Medieval Philosophy and Theology* 2 (1992): 53–73.

3. *ST* 1a, q. 22, a. 1, resp.

4. *ST* 1a, q. 22, a. 1, resp.

5. *ST* 1a, q. 22, a. 2, resp.

6. *ST* 1a, q. 22, a. 2 ad 4.

7. *ST* 1a, q. 22, a. 2 ad 4.

8. *ST* 1a2ae, prologue.

9. *ST* 1a2ae, q. 3, a. 8, resp. I return to this discussion again in much greater detail in ch. 4.

10. *ST* 1a2ae, q. 90, prologue.

11. *ST* 1a2ae, q. 90, a. 1–4.

12. *ST* 1a2ae, q. 93, a. 3, resp.

13. *ST* 1a2ae, q. 91, a. 1–4.

14. *ST* 1a2ae, q. 91, a. 1, resp.

15. *ST* 1a2ae, q. 93, a. 1, resp.

16. *ST* 1a2ae, q. 93, a. 5, resp.

17. *ST* 1a2ae, q. 91, a. 2, resp.

18. *ST* 1a2ae, q. 91, a. 2, resp.: "per quam habet naturalem inclinationem ad debitum actum et finem."

19. *ST* 1a2ae, q. 91, a. 2, resp.

20. *ST* 1a2ae, q. 90, prologue.

21. *ST* 1a2ae, q. 91, a. 2, resp.

22. *ST* 1a2ae, q. 90, a. 4 ad 1.

23. See especially the very fine essay by Thomas Hibbs, "Divine Irony and the Natural Law Speculation and Edification in Aquinas," *International Philosophical Quarterly* 30, no. 4 (December 1990): 419–29. This essay has helped me to see more clearly the "reflexive" aspect of the work of the natural law. I will discuss my differences with Hibbs's argument, especially regarding the Old Law, in the next chapter. Alasdair MacIntyre also deploys, in discussing Aquinas, a notion of practical reasoning as a kind of self-education in his *Whose Justice?* (177–82).

24. *ST* 1a2ae, q. 93, a. 5, resp.

25. See *ST* 2a2ae, q. 48–49, for Thomas on prudence. I return to this issue later on in my argument. It will be clear even at this point, however, how my argument is in accord with Nelson's *Priority*

of Prudence, discussed in the first chapter: prudence absolutely is required for knowing how to achieve our good. Where I differ from Nelson is in my interpretation of how the natural law informs and guides prudence.

26. *ST* 1a2ae, q. 94, a. 1.

27. *ST* 1a2ae, q. 94, a. 6, resp.: "Quantum ergo ad illa principia communia, lex naturalis nullo modo potest a cordibus hominum deleri in universali." Aquinas's earlier discussion of *synderesis* in the *Summa* occurs in 1a, q. 79, a. 12. In this article, he argues that *synderesis* gives us first principles in action so that "we proceed in discovering and we judge about what we have discovered" (a. 12, resp.).

28. *ST* 1a2ae, q. 94, a. 2, resp.

29. *ST* 1a2ae, q. 94, a. 1, sed contra.

30. 1a2ae, q. 94, a. 2, resp.

31. *ST* 1a, q. 79, a. 12 ad 3: "The unchanging *rationes* of this kind are the first principles of action (*operabilium*), about which one does not err; and these [*rationes*] are attributed to reason as a potency and to *synderesis* as a habit."

32. *ST* 1a2ae, q. 10 and q. 18 especially.

33. I grant that this explanation of *synderesis* makes Aquinas's claim of *synderesis*'s freedom from error peculiar. It may just be peculiar. For a useful discussion of *synderesis* and the knowledge it gives, see Mark D. Jordan's *Ordering Wisdom: The Hierarchy of Philosophical Discourses in Aquinas* (Notre Dame, Ind.: University of Notre Dame Press, 1986), 140–41.

Oscar J. Brown also has a helpful appendix on *synderesis* in Aquinas: see *Natural Rectitude and Divine Law in Aquinas* (Toronto: Pontifical Institute of Mediaeval Studies, 1981), 175–77. Although Brown becomes caught up in the, on my view, red herring of the is/ought problem, still his explanation of how the *inclinationes* are known is subtle and textually attentive (see *Natural Rectitude*, 31–37).

34. Witness the cottage industry John Finnis and Germain Grisez have built up in explaining the first principles within *synderesis*.

35. Thus I take Thomas's use of *synderesis* to be significant. M. B. Crowe takes a very different view in *The Changing Profile of the Natural Law* (The Hague: Martinus Nijhoff, 1977): "It is clear then, that, by the time he came to write his *Summa theologiae*, St. Thomas no longer regarded *synderesis* as a term of importance" (140). Crowe states that this is so in part because of Thomas's more complete

understanding of Aristotle's *Nicomachean Ethics*, in which practical wisdom's attention to particulars is given special emphasis. But I see no necessary tension between Thomas's use of *synderesis* as I have sketched it and the influence of Aristotle. Aristotle also admits of first principles in his *Ethics*, and these principles are enriched and supplemented in ethical inquiry.

36. *ST* 1a2ae, q. 94, a. 6, resp. It may occur to one that such a claim is easy to make but hard to prove; I suspect the only sort of proof possible would be phenomenological in kind. Simone Weil, in her writings about the "human personality," might provide a good example of such a proof. See *Simone Weil Reader*, ed. George A. Panichas (New York: Moyer Bell Limited, 1977), 313–39.

As both Jean Porter and Daniel Mark Nelson note, there is no determination of the will to specific objects, even to the goods of the *inclinationes* (see Jean Porter, *The Recovery of Virtue: The Relevance of Aquinas for Christian Ethics* [Louisville: Westminster/John Knox Press, 1990], 88; and Nelson, *Priority*, 47). One may understand by this claim first that the goods to which we are naturally inclined may be achieved in a variety of ways and social forms; there is no set determination of our nature to one specific form of achievement. Also, Porter argues further that human beings who do not so desire some good to which humans are inclined are not a "logical impossibility" (*Recovery*, 88) because "natural dynamisms may fail to function in a particular case" (ibid). She cites *ST* 1a, q. 49, a. 3 ad 5, in this regard; but Thomas here assigns the cause for evil in humanity as a conflict between reason and sensuality. This does not seem to be as much a failure in natural dynamism as a moral failure.

37. *ST* 1a2ae, q. 94. a. 2, resp.

38. *ST* 1a2ae, q. 94, a. 2, resp.

39. *ST* 1a2ae, q. 94, a. 2, resp.

40. For a clear discussion of inclusive versus monolithic conceptions of human happiness, see J. L. Ackrill's "Aristotle on *Eudaimonia*," in *Essays on Aristotle's Ethics*, ed. Amélie Oksenberg Rorty (Berkeley: University of California Press, 1980), 17–18. Although the discussion bears on Aristotle's characterization of the human end, it is applicable to Thomas's as well.

41. I agree with Nelson that Thomas, in his discussion of the natural law and sexuality, can fall prey to "a crude kind of physical naturalism" (*Priority*, 122). Nelson makes this remark about Thomas's out-of-hand condemnation of homosexuality in q. 94, a.

3 ad 2, and I think Nelson is correct in his judgment. I make this point to raise the issue, not addressed by Thomas, of whether the inflexible linking, or even the equation, of the goods of sexuality with procreation is an impoverished way of deliberating about this particular *inclinatio*.

42. And Thomas's tiers of inclinations mirror the levels of capacities in the Aristotelian soul: nutritive, animal, and rational. See *De Anima* II and III.

43. In my reading of this passage, it will be clear that I agree with the claim Porter makes in *Recovery of Virtue*, 85–91. She reads Thomas's remarks about the *inclinationes* as "his theory about the natural human good" (89). It will also be clear in what way, then, I am in substantial disagreement with Nelson's claim, discussed above in ch. 1, that the natural law functions in Aquinas only as a formal explanation of action. Rather, the natural law, when adequately reasoned about and known, functions as a normative standard for natural human flourishing.

44. *ST* 1a2ae, q. 94, a. 4, resp. My translation here relies on the English Dominican Fathers' translation.

45. *ST* 1a2ae, q. 94, a. 4, resp.

46. *ST* 1a2ae, q. 94, a. 6, resp.

47. I am not attributing to Thomas some radical version of this claim: it is fairly clear that he puts constraints on, for example, the "proper" structure of the family. Look at how he plays this understanding out when he treats of the order of charity, 2a2ae, q. 26. Still, Thomas does manifest an awareness of how customs can vary in different communities and how this variance does not necessarily call the universality of natural law into question.

I also am not, in speaking of a certain permissible variance in the forms of flourishing, repudiating a natural hierarchy to the goods constitutive of human flourishing This will be clearer in what I say below about how social forms and practices can obscure knowledge of the natural law.

48. Thomas of course mentions idolatry as one corrupt practice which the Old Law is intended to supplant; this will be discussed at length in the next chapter.

49. I wish to thank Mark Jordan for helping me formulate this claim more clearly.

50. I take our experience itself to be narrative in structure, viz., intelligible not as discrete moments or events but as sequential and

layered, with later choices and projects understood, even experienced, in the light of what has come before and what is projected to lie ahead. This is obviously only the beginning of a definition. I also take the process of learning the natural law to be itself narrative in the way I have described: progressive, drawing on experience. Ch. 5 takes up this argument in greater detail.

For a fine introduction into the kind of phenomenological inquiry that must ground ultimately any claim for the narrative nature of human experience, see Stephen Crites's essay, "The Narrative Quality of Experience," *Journal of the American Academy of Religion* 39, no. 3 (September 1971): 291–311.

For another position on natural law as serving to constitute a specific form of life, see Stanley Hauerwas's "Natural Law, Tragedy and Ethics," *Truthfulness and Tragedy: Further Investigations into Christian Ethics* (Notre Dame, Ind.: University of Notre Dame Press, 1977), 57–70, especially 64–67.

51. That is to say, practical reasoning about these matters is in part the work of prudence. I am not intending any loaded references to neo-Thomistic debates about the practical syllogism.

52. I thank Mark Jordan of the University of Notre Dame for helping me to formulate this point.

53. See MacIntyre's discussion of Thomistic prudence, *Whose Justice?* 196–97, to which I am indebted for this point.

54. *ST* 1a, q. 22, a. 2 ad 4. Note also that *providentia* and *prudentia* are linked etymologically. I make exactly this point as well in my critique of Goerner ("Goerner on Thomistic Natural Law," 645).

55. I take an example from the Decalogue. Thomas notes in the *Summa*, 1a2ae, q. 100, a. 1, that the moral precepts of the Old Law really amount to the natural law.

56. It will be clear from these remarks that I agree with Nelson that prudence and the moral virtues are central to Thomas's moral theology. But also central is Thomas's doctrine of natural law.

57. *ST* 2a2ae, q. 47, a. 1 and 2.

58. *ST* 2a2ae, q. 47, a. 15, resp.

59. *ST* 2a2ae, q. 47, a. 3, resp.

60. *ST* 1a2ae, q. 94, a. 4, resp., for example.

61. *ST* 1a2ae, q. 47, a. 2.

62. *ST* 2a2ae, q. 47, a. 6 ad 1; cf. *ST* 1a, q. 79, a. 12.

63. *ST* 2a2ae, q. 47, a. 6 ad 3. Nelson notices this passage (*Priority*, 96), but he ultimately interprets it as "serv[ing] the function

of explaining how we begin to reason practically" (ibid., 97). He notes that *synderesis* cannot "provide content for moral deliberations" (ibid., 97). On his view, only prudence can do this; thus he still neglects to treat of natural law as more than a formal explanation for action.

64. This is a task which is not always easy. Witness contemporary debates on the ethical status of abortion, capital punishment, and nuclear deterrence.

65. *ST* 2a2ae, q. 48, a. 1, resp.

66. *ST* 2a2ae, q. 49, a. 1–8.

67. *ST* 2a2ae, q. 49, a. 3, resp.

68. *ST* 1a2ae, q. 95, a. 2, resp. The English Dominican Fathers' translation guides my own.

69. Ibid.

70. *ST* 1a2ae, q. 96, a. 4, resp.

71. *ST* 1a2ae, q. 92, a. 1, resp.

72. *ST* 1a2ae, q. 94, a. 3, resp., and q. 96, a. 3, resp. Not all the vices, however, are punished under human law, lest the law become too burdensome and contempt for it be taught (q. 96, a. 2, resp. and ad 2).

73. *ST* 1a2ae, q. 91, a. 4, resp.

74. *ST* 1a2ae, q. 91, a. 6, resp.

3. Natural Law and the Old Law

1. *ST* 1a2ae, q. 91, a. 4, resp.

2. *ST* 1a2ae, q. 91, a. 4, resp.

3. *ST* 1a2ae, q. 94, a. 2, resp.

4. The additional three reasons given in the *responsio* of *ST* 1a2ae, q. 91, a. 4, underscore further inadequacies in human law (even informed by natural law); these pertain to the error to which human judgment is prone and to human law's inability to regulate interior movements of the soul and to punish all evils.

5. I discuss Thomas's treatment of the human end in greater detail in ch. 4, within the context of the New Law.

6. In the present chapter, I make specific references to points in Hibbs's argument in "Divine Irony," but here I would like more generally to credit the help I have received from his close and attentive reading of Thomas on the Old Law. Also of help for those

interested in exploring the connections between natural and divine law are: Brown's *Natural Rectitude*; and F. Russell Hittinger's "Aquinas' Doctrine of Natural Law: An Account of Morality?" paper presented at the meetings of the American Catholic Philosophical Association, Boston, 1991. This latter paper also takes up E. A. Goerner's reading of natural law; Hittinger emphasizes, as do I, the theological dimension of Thomistic ethics. I thank Professor Goerner for making the paper available to me.

On the connection between natural and divine law, Hibbs puts it, "The movement from natural to divine law, then, has a teleological intelligibility; that is, the aspirations of the natural law, which are identical to the goals of human nature, are realized only in divine law" ("Divine Irony," 423).

7. *ST* 1a2ae, q. 98, a. 1, resp.

8. *ST* 1a2ae, q. 98, a. 1, resp.

9. *ST* 1a2ae, q. 98, a. 1, resp.

10. *ST* 1a2ae, q. 98, a. 1 ad 1.

11. *ST* 1a2ae, q. 98, a. 1 ad 2.

12. *ST* 1a2ae, q. 98, a. 2, resp.

13. *ST* 1a2ae, q. 98, a. 2 ad 3. Following the Blackfriars Dominican translation (Blackfriars: Eyre and Spotiswoode, 1965).

14. See Hibbs, "Divine Irony," 426–27.

15. See *ST* 1a2ae, q. 98, a. 5, resp., and q. 100, a. 1, resp. Thomas speaks of the moral precepts commanding acts of virtue in q. 99, a. 2, resp.

16. *ST* 1a2ae, q. 98, a. 6, resp.

17. *ST* 1a2ae, q. 98, a. 6, resp.

18. Thus I do not take the work of the Old Law to be purely cognitive, as does, for example, Brown, in *Natural Rectitude*, where he argues that the Old Law was good "as a matter of cognitive completion but not necessarily of operative efficacy" (118). Brown emphasizes the stricter obligations incurred with written law, but he does not connect this with Thomas's remarks about teaching humility to the Jews. Brown discusses an interesting related text of Thomas's, his commentary on *Romans*.

19. *ST* 1a2ae, q. 98, a. 6 ad 1. Thomas repeats the word *nondum* (not yet) twice, in each part of his claim, thereby emphasizing the temporal nature of his claim.

20. *ST* 1a2ae, q. 99, a. 2 ad 2.

21. See Hibbs, "Divine Irony," 425, for much the same point.

But while Hibbs emphasizes the individual's reappropriation of the natural law (429), I take Thomas to place primary stress on the community's role in obscuring or clarifying the natural law for its members.

22. Hittinger uses similar language in describing the natural law in his paper, "Aquinas' Doctrine of Law," 28.

23. *ST* 1a2ae, q. 94, a. 6, resp.

24. See Hibbs, "Divine Irony," 424, on this education of the Jews as a kind of "recollection."

25. *ST* 1a2ae, q. 99, a. 6, resp.

26. *ST* 1a2ae, q. 99, a. 6 ad 1 and ad 2.

27. This ultimate goal the Old Law could not accomplish by itself, as I argue later in this chapter.

28. Although Aquinas does remark that the moral precepts are binding for all, because they are equivalent to the natural law (*ST* 1a2ae, q. 98, a. 5, resp.).

29. See for example *ST* 1a2ae, q. 98, a. 1; q. 99, a. 3; q. 100, a. 2.

30. *ST* 1a2ae, q. 99, a. 2, resp.

31. *ST* 1a2ae, q. 99, a. 2, resp. (following English Dominican Fathers' translation).

32. *ST* 1a2ae, q. 99, a. 3 ad 2. I will follow Aquinas's own practice of using the present tense in describing the relations between precepts.

33. *ST* 1a2ae, q. 99, a. 3, resp.

34. *ST* 1a2ae, q. 99, a. 4, resp.

35. Thomas treats of the ceremonial precepts in *ST* 1a2ae, q. 101–103, and of the judicial precepts in *ST* 1a2ae, q. 104–105.

36. *ST* 1a2ae, q. 101, a. 3, resp.

37. *ST* 1a2ae, q. 98, a. 6, resp. This article was discussed above.

38. *ST* 1a2ae, q. 101, a. 3, resp.

39. *ST* 1a2ae, q. 104, a. 4, resp. Hibbs, in "Divine Irony," apparently neglects the pedagogical function of the ceremonial and judicial precepts. Likewise, he does not indicate that these precepts, too, are determinations of the natural law, although in a different sense from the moral precepts (see "Divine Irony," 422).

40. *ST* 1a2ae, q. 99, a. 2, resp.

41. *ST* 1a2ae, q. 100, a. 2, resp.

42. *ST* 1a2ae, q. 100, a. 2, resp.

43. *ST* 1a2ae, q. 100, a. 1, sed contra.

44. *ST* 1a2ae, q. 100, a. 1, resp.

45. All quotations in this paragraph come from *ST* 1a2ae, q. 100, a. 1, resp.

46. *ST* 1a2ae, q. 100, a. 3, resp. The discussion that follows, including quotations, is drawn from this article unless otherwise noted.

47. *ST* 1a2ae, q. 100, a. 3, resp.

48. *ST* 1a2ae, q. 100, a. 4, resp.

49. *ST* 1a2ae, q. 100, a. 4, resp.

50. *ST* 1a2ae, q. 100, a. 5, resp. All references and quotations in this paragraph are from this source unless otherwise noted.

51. *ST* 1a2ae, q. 100, a. 5 ad 1.

52. *ST* 1a2ae, q. 100, a. 8, resp. References in the paragraph that follows, including quotations, are from this source unless noted otherwise.

53. *ST* 1a2ae, q. 100, a. 8, resp.

54. *ST* 1a2ae, q. 94, a. 3, resp., and q. 100, a. 2, resp.

55. *ST* 1a2ae, q. 100, a. 8 ad 2.

56. *ST* 1a2ae, q. 100, a. 9, resp.

57. *ST* 1a2ae, q. 100, a. 9 ad 2.

58. *ST* 1a2ae, q. 100, a. 10 ad 2.

59. *ST* 1a2ae, q. 100, a. 10 ad 3.

60. *ST* 1a2ae, q. 100, a. 12, resp

61. *ST* 1a2ae, q. 100, a. 1, resp.

62. *ST* 1a2ae, q. 98, a. 4, resp.

63. See Hibbs, "Divine Irony," 424, on sin as a "disease of forgetfulness."

64. Although Thomas repeatedly emphasizes the inadequacy of the Old Law, he tempers this claim for some individuals living at the time of the Old Covenant (in *ST* 1a2ae, q. 107, a. 1 ad 2): "Having charity and the grace of the Holy Spirit," such persons were moved to virtue "because of the love of virtue," by spiritual promises alone; that is, they had moved beyond the Old Law's pedagogy of temporal rewards or punishments. Thomas takes their love of spiritual things for their own sake as evidence of the connaturality of charity within them. Such spiritual promises are "objects of the virtues, chiefly of charity. And so such people were inclined in themselves to those [promises], not as though to something alien, but as to something proper to them."

In so loving spiritual things alone, such persons belonged to the New Law, even though they lived before the entrance of Christ into human history. Thomas cites Moses, in a quotation from Paul, as an example of such a person (*ST* 1a2ae, q. 107, a. 1 ad 3). Thomas also refers to the "implicit faith" of those living at the time of the Old Law but belonging to the New Law, at *ST* 1a2ae, q 106, a. 1 ad 3, and a. 3 ad 2.

4. Natural Law and the New Law

1. In the discussion that follows, I am indebted to the work of Kevin Staley and Jean Porter. See Kevin M. Staley, "Happiness: The Natural End of Man?" *Thomist* 53, no. 2 (April 1989): 215–34. Staley provides a valuable history of debate in this century on whether Thomas in fact allows for a natural, albeit imperfect, human end. He argues persuasively that Thomas must and does teach that there is an end proportionate to our powers of attainment because the concept of a nature for Aquinas requires an end to which that nature is directed by specific potencies (231–32).

Jean Porter takes up Staley's conclusions in *Recovery of Virtue*, 63–68. She builds on them to offer an account of how the natural human end functions in moral reasoning, even within the order of grace See also her article "Desire for God: Ground of the Moral Life in Aquinas," *Theological Studies* 47 (1986)· 48–68, especially 54–65.

2. *ST* 1a2ae, q. 1, a. 1.

3. *ST* 1a2ae, q. 1, a 4.

4. *ST* 1a2ae, q. 1, a 6.

5. See Alan Donagan's use of this distinction in his *Human Ends and Human Actions· An Exploration in St. Thomas's Treatment*, Aquinas Lecture, 1985 (Milwaukee: Marquette University Press, 1985), 6–17.

6. *ST* 1a2ae, q. 1, a. 8, resp.

7. *ST* 1a, q. 44, a. 4, resp.: "For every creature intends to pursue its own perfection, which is the similitude of divine goodness and perfection. In this way divine goodness is the end of all things." See also *ST* 1a, q. 44, a. 4 ad 3.

8. See Jean Porter's exposition of this point in Thomas ("Desire for God," 50–55).

9. Thomas employs precisely this distinction of capacities in describing the differing modes of participation in the eternal law by the

irrational and rational creature. See *ST* 1a2ae, q. 91, a. 2, resp. and ad 3. Thomas distinguishes how irrational creatures participate in the eternal law, only by a kind of similitude through being directed to their "proper acts and ends," from the manner in which rational creatures share in it.

10. *ST* 1a2ae, q. 2, a. 8, resp.

11. *ST* 1a2ae, q. 2, a. 7, resp.

12. *ST* 1a2ae, q. 5, a. 8, resp. Thomas's claim that God is our perfect and complete good does not involve him in the additional claim that all *do* in fact actually desire God. Thomas takes men and women to hold many mistaken notions of what would constitute their ultimate happiness.

13. *ST* 1a2ae, q. 5, a. 3, resp.

14. *ST* 1a2ae, q. 5, a. 3, resp.

15. Indeed, Alan Donagan describes as "tragic" Aristotle's view of human life (*Human Ends*, 19); see also his discussion of how Aquinas transforms Aristotelian *eudaimonia* (*Human Ends*, 28–39, especially 38–39).

16. *ST* 1a2ae, q. 4, a. 7 and 8. Indeed, Thomas reads the material promises of Scripture as "metaphorical," signifying the enjoyment we will find in the possession of God (q. 4, a. 7 ad 1). Thomas does allow for the love of friends in charity to be a possible "concomitant" happiness (q. 4, a. 8 ad 3).

17. See also Thomas's remarks about the constraints of sensory knowledge in attempting to understand the immaterial (*ST* 1a, q. 88, a. 1 and 2).

18. *ST* 1a2ae, q. 3, a. 6 ad 3.

19. See, for example, Thomas's own "ways" of reasoning towards God at the beginning of the *Summa theologiae*, 1a, q. 2, a. 3. These five arguments have typically been badly misrepresented in traditional pedagogy (as demonstrations); their conclusions are best considered as descriptions which converge toward God: e.g., "which is what all call God"; "and this is what we call God"; and "this all understand to be God." Louis Mackey's essay on the five ways is particularly helpful: "Entreatments of God," *Franciscan Studies* 37 (1977): 103–19.

On the inconceivability of God except in the beatific vision, see David B. Burrell's discussion in *Aquinas: God and Action* (Notre Dame, Ind.: University of Notre Dame Press, 1979), part 1. Porter also has a clear statement of Thomas's position on true happiness and the ensuing problems for practical reason ("Desire for God," 55–56).

20. *ST* 1a2ae, q. 5, a. 5, resp. (I follow the English Dominican Fathers' translation for *deficit* as "falls short").

21. *ST* 1a2ae, q. 3, a. 8, resp. Thomas cites in this regard Aristotle's claim (*Metaphysics* 1, 2) that philosophy began with wonder.

22. *ST* 1a2ae, q. 5, a. 5 ad 1.

23. *ST* 1a2ae, q. 106, a. 1, resp.

24. *ST* 1a2ae, q. 106, a. 1 ad 2 (I follow the English Dominican Fathers' translation of *inditum* as "instilled").

25. *ST* 1a2ae, q. 106, a. 2, sed contra and resp.

26. *ST* 1a2ae, q. 110, a. 1, resp.

27. *ST* 1a2ae, q. 112, a. 1, resp.

28. *ST* 1a2ae, q. 110, a. 3 ad 3.

29. *ST* 1a2ae, q. 106, a. 1 ad 1.

30 *ST* 1a2ae, q. 108, a. 1 ad 1.

31 *ST* 1a2ae, q. 108, a. 2, resp.

32. *ST* 1a2ae, q. 108, a. 3, resp. All subsequent quotations in this paragraph derive from this passage unless otherwise noted.

In this discussion, as in much of his treatment of the New Law, Thomas cites Augustine as his chief and guiding authority. His exposition acknowledges Augustine's own discussion of the Sermon on the Mount. Note, too, that Thomas is not speaking here only of what is commonly called the Beatitudes (Matt. 5:1–12); his exegesis encompasses all of Matt. 5–7.

33. See Matt. 5:8–9, 13–14; Matt. 6:28 (trans. of Revised Standard Version [New York: Oxford University Press, 1962]).

34. *ST* 1a2ae, q. 108, a. 2 ad 3. Speaking here of the apostles, Thomas explicitly acknowledges that Christ removes the constraints of specific "modes of living" connected with the ritual observances of the Old Law. They were left "totally to their own choice in those things which did not belong necessarily to virtue."

35. *ST* 1a2ae, q. 106, a. 2, resp.

36. *ST* 1a2ae, q. 107, a. 4, resp.

37. *ST* 1a2ae, q 107, a. 1, resp.

38. *ST* 1a2ae, q. 106, a. 3, resp.

39. *ST* 1a2ae, q. 107, a. 2, resp. Thomas also reads the Sermon on the Mount in the light of the New Law's fulfillment of the Old Law. Aquinas takes Christ in the Sermon to display the way to completion

of the Old Law as well as a correction of the Pharisees' interpretation of it (see *ST* 1a2ae, q. 108, a. 3 ad 1–3). Thus these words of Christ, which provide for Thomas a comprehensive representation of the Christian life, are interpreted in the light of their historical significance for the Jews. The Sermon comprises not only teachings about what is necessary for salvation but also counsels targeted to correct interpretive distortions of the Old Law.

40. *ST* 1a2ae, q. 107, a. 2 ad 1. Thomas also acknowledges that the judicial precepts fail to bind, because the civil authority from which they derived is no more (see *ST* 1a2ae, q. 104, a. 3).

Thomas explains (in the *responsio* of q. 107, a. 2) how Christ fulfilled the Old Law in his teaching: first by extending the sense of the commandments to include "interior dispositions" and not merely the external act, as, for example, in the case of adultery. Aquinas calls this extension the "true understanding" (*verum intellectum*) of the Old Law. Christ also teaches how to keep the precepts more "safely" or surely, by abstaining from occasions of sin. Lastly, Christ "superadds" certain counsels of perfection: Thomas cites the rich young man of Matt. 19, who is told to sell all he has if he wishes to be perfect.

41. *ST* 1a2ae, q. 106, a. 4, resp. Thomas acknowledges another sense of the New Law which can vary from time and place: how the New Law, as grace, is possessed and enacted by different men and women. Thomas compares this variation to the variation in enactment of the Old Law among the Jews.

42. See Stanley Hauerwas on how to understand the effect of grace in the life of the Christian ("Natural Law, Tragedy, and Ethics," in *Truthfulness and Tragedy*, especially 66–68). He speaks of grace's transformation of "self" or "character" as the most accurate description of its effect on believers.

43. *ST* 1a2ae, q. 58, a. 1–3: Thomas distinguishes between the moral and intellectual "human" virtues.

44. *ST* 1a2ae, q. 62, a. 1, resp.

45. *ST* 1a2ae, q. 62, a. 3, resp.

46. *ST* 1a2ae, q. 66, a. 6, resp.

47. *ST* 1a2ae, q. 67, a. 6 ad 3; see *ST* 1a2ae, q. 67, a. 3–5, for his discussion of the status of faith and hope after this life.

48. *ST* 2a2ae, q. 23, a. 7, resp.

49. *ST* 2a2ae, q. 23, a. 8 ad 3.

50. *ST* 1a2ae, q. 65, a. 4, resp.

51. *ST* 1a, q. 12, a. 11 and 12.

52. See Porter, "Desire for God," 63: "The love of charity begins where our cognitive knowledge of God ends."

53. *ST* 1a2ae, q. 66, a. 6 ad 1. See F. Russell Hittinger's useful explanation of this claim (also in relation to charity): "When It Is More Excellent to Love than to Know: The Other Side of Thomistic 'Realism'," *Proceedings of the American Catholic Philosophical Association*, 57 (1983): 171–79.

Thomas invokes this claim in his more detailed treatment of charity in the secunda secundae as well: "According to this it should be argued that love, which is an act of the appetitive power, even in this state of life tends first to God, and from him turns to other things. In this way charity loves God immediately and other things through God. In cognition it is in fact the converse, because we know God through other things, as a cause through an effect or by mode of eminence or negation" (*ST* 2a2ae, q. 27, a. 4, resp.).

54. *ST* 1a2ae, q. 4, a. 2 and 3: The vision of God is primary for beatitude; delight follows upon vision.

55. John 15:15 (trans. as quoted by Thomas in *ST* 2a2ae, q. 23, a. 1, sed contra).

56. *ST* 1a2ae, q. 65, a. 5, resp.

57. *ST* 2a2ae, q. 23, a. 1 ad 1 Thomas is quoting the Vulgate translation of Philippians 3:20; this citation seems to be, among his authorities, the source for his use of *conversatio* as a way of speaking of our union with God. The word carries both the sense of conversation as communication and a more comprehensive meaning as the place or act of dwelling-with (Lewis and Short, *Latin Dictionary*, [Oxford: Oxford University Press, 1969], 464a). Aquinas uses the word in both senses to speak of charity as friendship. It serves, in Philippians, as a translation for the Greek *politeuma*.

58. *ST* 2a2ae, q. 45, a. 2, resp.

59. *ST* 2a2ae, q. 45, a. 3, resp.

60. See Jean Porter, "*De Ordine Caritatis*: Charity, Friendship, and Justice in Thomas Aquinas' *Summa Theologiae*," *Thomist* 53 (April 1989): 197–213. She sketches Thomas's appropriation of Aristotle in his use of the relation of friendship to describe charity.

61. Aristotle, *Nicomachean Ethics* 1159b1–5.

62. Aristotle, *Nicomachean Ethics* 1159a35–1159b3.

63. Aristotle, *Nicomachean Ethics* 1159a5–12.

64. *ST* 2a2ae, q. 27, a. 7.

65. Aristotle, *Nicomachean Ethics* 1177b25–1178a2. Amélie Oksenberg Rorty argues for a substantially different understanding of contemplation from what I sketch here, in her fine essay, "The Place of Contemplation in Aristotle's *Nicomachean Ethics*," in *Essays on Aristotle's Ethics*, ed. Amélie Oksenberg Rorty (Berkeley: University of California Press, 1980), 377–94. She supplies content to Aristotle's essentially formal description of the activity of *theoria*. As contemplators, we contemplate "Humanity" and its "essential *energeiai*," on her view. Indeed, Rorty offers a kind of reconciliation of the goods of friendship and contemplation internal to Aristotle's ethics itself. While this interpretation is attractive for its connection of what look to be disparate claims in Aristotle's ethics, I do not find persuasive her root interpretation of *theoria* as thought about virtuous human beings. Such being is not the highest actuality of which Aristotle speaks, and it is unlikely then that reflection on them constitutes the highest thought of which humans are capable.

66. Thomas uses the quotation I recapitulate here in part, from 1 John 3:2, in the sed contra of *ST* 1a2ae, q. 3, a. 8. He argues here for *beatitudo* as the vision of the divine essence.

67. In saying what I do about *theoria* in Aristotle's ethics, I am not indicating that I take contemplation to be in any sole sense *eudaimonia* for Aristotle. Whether Aristotle holds an inclusive or a monolithic conception of the human end is of course a much debated topic, and I alluded to the controversy in ch. 2, in my presentation of Thomas's account of the natural human end. To state my own view most simply: I take Aristotle to hold a conception of flourishing which includes *theoria* as well as other goods, including social goods, the practice of the moral virtues, and certain material goods. A life in pursuit of *theoria* alone, although it is the activity most desirable for its own sake, is impracticable, as well as unsuitable, for human beings according to Aristotle. Nancy Sherman, in her excellent discussion of contemplation and the human good in *Fabric* (94–106), argues persuasively that it must be *phronesis* that will precisely deliberate about when and how the virtuous person is to pursue the various goods, among them contemplation, that are constitutive of flourishing (*Fabric*, 101–3).

Might prudence and contemplation be related in Aquinas in a similar way? Thomas does of course take contemplation of God to be the human end, as I have discussed. At the end of the secunda secundae, Thomas compares the respective merits of the contemplative and active lives. Thomas treats of contemplation in this regard as a choice of life ordered primarily towards the pursuit of contemplation of God, hindered in this life by both sensuality and our natural epistemic constraints. Aristotle does not, I believe, endorse such a single-minded practice of *theoria*, precisely because of his different conception of the human end. Aquinas, for his part, indicates that the contemplative life is intrinsically more excellent (*ST* 2a2ae, q. 182, a. 1, resp.) than the active life. The moral virtues dispose a person towards contemplation (*ST* 2a2ae, q. 180, a. 2). The active life can aid in contemplation by "quieting and ordering" the interior passions of the soul which can impede contemplation (*ST* 2a2ae, q. 182, a. 3, resp.). Prudence most properly belongs to the active life because it acquires its end from the moral virtues, but it can at least aid by disposing towards contemplation (*ST* 2a2ae, q. 181, a. 1 ad 3, and q. 181, a. 2, resp.). Still, it is the gift of counsel, corresponding to prudence, which gives a person knowledge from the Spirit "of all things which are ordered to the end of eternal life" (*ST* 2a2ae, q. 52, a. 4 ad 2). This special perfection of prudence can certainly be understood to contribute to such decisions as whether to pursue an active or contemplative life. In this way, one might say that prudence plays a part even in Thomas in determining how and when the goods of human life are to be pursued.

68. *ST* 2a2ae, q. 45, a. 3, resp. Thomas is guided in this discussion by Augustine's description of wisdom in *De Trinitate* XII.

69. Thomas, when treating of the active and contemplative lives later in the secunda secundae, distinguishes and at the same time links them. Both require the moral virtues, although in different ways; both are ordered to the expression of charity, although in different ways. While Thomas takes the contemplative life to be intrinsically more meritorious, because it is ordered directly to the contemplation of God, the active life still disposes to contemplation (see *ST* 2a2ae, q. 179–82). Thus Thomas does not, even when speaking of states of life, separate utterly the loving attentiveness to God (in contemplation) which is the work of charity and the solicitude and affection for neighbor which is charity's secondary work.

70. *ST* 2a2ae, q. 45, a. 6, resp. (there is no satisfying, inclusive way to render *ad Dei filiationem*; thus I follow the English Dominican Fathers' translation as "sonship to God").

71. *ST* 2a2ae, q. 45, a. 6 ad 3.

72. See Porter's "*De Ordine Caritatis*," on the integrating function of charity: "It follows that for Thomas, charity functions as the supreme organizing principle in the personality of the justified, by which not only all of their actions, but all their desires and impulses, are directed to God" (204). I am indebted to her clear exegesis of this point. I also use the term the *justified* to refer to those within the life of grace.

73. See *ST* 1a, q. 12, a. 12, resp., and q. 12, a. 13 ad 1. Thomas argues that we can, by natural reason, know that God exists and is first cause.

74. See Porter on this point in "Desire for God," 65–66, and *Recovery*, 65–67.

75. *ST* 2a2ae, q. 45, a. 2.

76. *ST* 1a2ae, q. 63, a. 3 ad 2.

77. See Thomas's remarks on concupiscence and the cause of sin in humankind (*ST* 1a2ae, q. 30; q. 77; q. 84, a. 1, resp.). His remarks presuppose an understanding of evil as a kind of privation of good; that is, evil in action involves a deficiency of some kind in the act (see *ST* 1a2ae, q. 18).

78 *ST* 1a2ae, q. 63, a. 4, resp.

79. See *ST* 1a2ae, q. 65, a. 3 ad 2 and 3. Note also that Thomas opposes to connatural wisdom (the special gift of the Spirit conferred by charity) *stultitia* (foolishness or folly). This foolishness is specifically a sin which "is a certain dullness (*stuporem*) in judging, principally about the highest cause, which is the ultimate end and greatest good. . . . [This sin is incurred when] man immerses his sense in earthly things, from which his sense is rendered inept at perceiving divine things" (*ST* 2a2ae, q. 46, a. 2, resp.). With the failure to enact a coherent and progressive love of God issues a consequent failure in understanding of what leads to God.

80. *ST* 1a2ae, q. 65, a. 2, resp.

81. *ST* 1a2ae, q. 63, a. 4, resp.

82. *ST* 1a2ae, q. 61, a. 1, resp.

83. *ST* 2a2ae, q. 47, a. 2 ad 1: "Wherefore it is manifest that prudence is wisdom regarding human things, but not wisdom *simpliciter* because it is not about the highest cause *simpliciter* but about the human good, which is not the best of that which is. And for this reason it is said significantly that prudence is wisdom for man, and not wisdom *simpliciter*."

84. *ST* 2a2ae, q. 47, a. 10, resp.

85. *ST* 2a2ae, q. 47, a. 10 ad 2. In arguing in this article against the restriction of prudence to care for one person's good only, Thomas responds that this position is repugnant to both charity and right reason. That is to say, in terms of both the natural and supernatural human ends, obligations exist towards the community.

Thomas distinguishes between kinds of prudence relative to different kinds of community in article 11 of the same question. Thomas names as different species of prudence political prudence, ordered to achieving the good of a political community; "economic" prudence, pertaining to the good of a family; and "monastic" prudence, pertaining to the good of a single individual.

86. *ST* 2a2ae, q. 47, a. 12, resp.

87. *ST* 2a2ae, q. 47, a. 13, resp.

88. *ST* 2a2ae, q. 47, a. 13, resp.

89. See *ST* 2a2ae, q. 47, a. 14, resp. and ad 3. See also *ST* 1a2ae, q. 65, a. 2, resp. Thomas discusses here infused prudence in the context of the work of charity, affirming that it requires charity to give it the ultimate end, possession of God; this is even more necessary to the *ratio* of prudence than the possession of the moral virtues, which dispose us well "with regard to other ends."

90. *ST* 2a2ae, q. 47, a. 14, obj. 1.

91. *ST* 2a2ae, q. 47, a. 14 ad 1. See also Thomas's remark about the acquired moral virtues at *ST* 1a2ae, q. 65, a. 3 ad 2: that they can promote greater ease in action (than the infused moral virtues) because the process of habituation eliminates "contrary dispositions." Presumably, these contrary dispositions remain and may be troublesome when the moral virtues are infused.

92. It is also counsel (*consilium*) that is the gift of the Holy Spirit corresponding to prudence; this gives understanding of what to do to achieve salvation (see *ST* 2a2ae, q. 52, a. 1 ad 2, and q. 52, a. 4 ad 2). Again, the end is supernatural.

93. *ST* 2a2ae, q. 47, a. 15, resp. See also same question, article 6, ad 1 and ad 3, for Aquinas's discussion of *synderesis* and prudence. I discuss this latter article in ch. 2.

94. *ST* 2a2ae, q. 50, a. 1–4.

95. See, for example, *ST* 2a2ae, q. 50, a. 2 ad 3, and q. 50, a. 3 ad 1.

96. *ST* 1a2ae, q. 65, a. 2, resp.

97. *ST* 1a2ae, q. 63, a. 4, resp.

98. See also Porter's discussion of political prudence in *Recovery*, 162–65.

99. *ST* 2a2ae, q. 52, a. 1 ad 1. Thomas has earlier described the gift of counsel as that which "perfects" the practical reason in its apprehension of truth (*ST* 1a2ae, q. 68, a. 4, resp.).

100. *ST* 2a2ae, q. 52, a. 1 ad 1, and a. 3, resp.

101. *ST* 2a2ae, q. 52, a. 1 ad 1.

102. *ST* 1a2ae, q. 96, a. 2 ad 2.

103. *ST* 2a2ae, q. 37 and 38.

104. *ST* 2a2ae, q. 39–42.

105. *ST* 2a2ae, q. 26, a. 6, resp. And see Porter, "De Ordine Caritatis," 205–6.

106. *ST* 2a2ae, q. 26, a. 13, sed contra.

107. See, for example, *ST* 1a, q. 1, a. 2 ad 2, on how "singulars" are employed in sacred doctrine as an example of a life (to be followed?) or as a declaration of the authority of those men through whom revelation comes. See also Christ as an example of virtue to be imitated (*ST* 3a, q. 15, a. 1). For an explanation of why we need examples to understand a truth, see *ST* 1a, q. 84, a. 7, resp.

108. Porter has argued that in fact "the specific natural ideal of morality remains the proximate goal of morality" (*Recovery*, 67). This is so, on her view, because we cannot base our practical reasoning upon a *telos* beyond our comprehension. But her argument fails to acknowledge what Thomas says about the mean of the acquired moral virtues being distinct from that of the infused moral virtues. She in fact claims that the two means have the "same normative content" ("*De ordine caritatis*," 211); but this is not what Thomas says. Likewise, Thomas makes a point of arguing for the necessity of infused prudence, as opposed to acquired prudence, for perfect virtue (*ST* 1a2ae, q. 65, a. 2); infused prudence sets a mean distinct from natural prudence.

Nonetheless, Porter is right to emphasize that the New Law does not render the natural law obsolete, and she is also correct in stressing that our attainment of God in charity is not cognitive. I acknowledge that these facts create problems for explaining, then, the precise way in which practical reason is guided within the New Law, and I do not pretend to have provided a complete answer here.

109. As Porter herself notes (*Recovery*, 67). She also examines the passage in *ST* 2a2ae, q. 29, a. 2 ad 4.

110. *ST* 2a2ae, q. 29, a. 2 ad 4.

111. *ST* 2a2ae, q. 29, a. 3, resp.

112. Thomas describes the increase and perfection of charity in just this way; see *ST* 2a2ae, q. 24, a. 7 and 8.

113. *ST* 2a2ae, q. 31–33

114. *ST* 2a2ae, q. 26, a. 13, resp.

115. *ST* 2a2ae, q. 26, a. 13, resp.

116. *ST* 2a2ae, q. 184, a. 2, resp. and ad 3, and q. 184, a. 3, resp.

117. *ST* 2a2ae, q. 186, a. 6 ad 2.

118. *ST* 2a2ae, q. 188, a. 8, resp. Thomas recalls Aristotle's *Politics* I, 1 ("Man is by nature a social animal") when speaking of one who withdraws from human community; when the motive is the desire to concentrate utterly on "divine things," rather than being like a beast, such a one is godlike (see *ST* 2a2ae, q. 188, a. 8 ad 5).

5. Practical Reasoning, Tragedy, and the Limits of the Natural Law

1. The work produced on this topic is immense and covers a wide range of positions. Some of the most prominent contributors, arguing for the realism of narrative form in describing the world, have been Barbara Hardy and Alasdair MacIntyre. See Hardy's essay, "The Nature of Narrative," in *The Collected Essays of Barbara Hardy*, vol. 1 (Sussex: Harvester Press, 1987), 1–13. See as well MacIntyre's remarks in "The Virtues, the Unity of a Human Life, and the Concept of a Tradition," ch. 15 of *After Virtue* (Notre Dame, Ind.: University of Notre Dame Press, 1981). MacIntyre's argument is not chiefly concerned with the question of how events are interpreted as narrative in structure, but he seems to presuppose, and to suggest, that there is a narrative structure to our experience of the world. He then goes on to argue for unity of the self defined as the unity of a life story In particular, MacIntyre wants to argue for a story in the form of a certain kind of quest or inquiry (203–4). In this sense, real "unity of life," real coherence, is in effect an achievement, not an inevitability. This is so because it is always possible, at least to some degree, to abandon the effort of a coherent life story committed to the projects he specifies.

Contributors arguing that human beings *impose* an artificial narrative structure on experience include Louis Mink and Hayden White.

See, for example, Mink's "Narrative Form as a Cognitive Instrument," in *The Writing of History: Literary Form and Historical Understanding*, ed. Robert Canary and Henry Kozicki (Madison: University of Wisconsin Press, 1978). Paul Ricoeur occupies a more hybrid position (see *Time and Narrative*, 3 vols., trans. Kathleen Blamey and David Pellauer [Chicago: University of Chicago Press, 1990]), but as David Carr argues, Ricoeur still seems to drive a wedge between narrative and the world it is supposed to describe and explain. For a philosophical position that argues for the continuity of narrative and the "world," see Carr's *Time, Narrative, and History* (Bloomington: Indiana University Press, 1986). Some of his claims are nicely summarized in his article, "Narrative and the Real World," *History and Theory* 25 (May 1986): 117–31.

2. See *ST* 1a, q. 10 on the eternity of God. The authority most frequently invoked as setting the terms of this discussion is Boethius, whose definition of eternity, from *The Consolation of Philosophy*, Thomas vindicates.

3. *ST* 1a, q. 10, a. 2 ad 1.

4. *ST* 1a, q. 10, a. 4 ad 2.

5. *ST* 1a, q. 10, a. 4 ad 3.

6. Some of the discussion of the Germans that follows is drawn from my article, "Goerner on Thomistic Natural Law," where my criticisms of Goerner are developed at greater length.

7. *ST* 1a2ae, q. 18, a. 1, resp.

8. Indeed Goerner's interpretation of natural law looks far less Thomistic than it does Hobbesian. The law curbs without improving, compelling obedience from fear rather than from any understanding or love.

9. And it is against the virtue of justice that robbery offends specifically (*ST* 2a2ae, q. 66, especially a. 8).

10. *ST* 2a2ae, q. 58, a. 1, resp.

11. *ST* 2a2ae, q. 66, a. 7, resp. Here Thomas argues that taking what is not one's own in order to sustain one's life is lawful and in accordance with the natural law. He does not deem such an action genuine theft or robbery.

12. *ST* 2a2ae, q. 66, a. 2 ad 1.

13. *ST* 2a2ae, q. 66, a. 2, resp., and q. 66, a 6, resp.

14. See *ST* 2a2ae, q. 66, a. 1–3.

15. In Caesar's own commentary, he says that the Germans valorized raiding on the grounds that it "exercised the youth and

diminished sloth" (*De Bello Gallico* VI, 23 [Oxford: Clarenden Press, 1951]). So, in correcting themselves, the Germans might decide that there are more appropriate means to these good ends.

16. See Carr's remarks in "Narrative and the Real World" on action as teleological and "future-oriented" (124).

17. Ralph McInerny, *Ethica Thomistica* (Washington, D.C.: Catholic University of America Press, 1982), 44.

18. Abigail Rosenthal, *A Good Look at Evil* (Philadelphia: Temple University Press, 1987), 13. Rosenthal uses the notion of narrative as a way of describing different sorts of evil human "types."

19. See *ST* 1a, q. 79, a. 8, resp The textual variant for *acquisitionis* is *inquisitionis*. Either reading, or both, supports my argument.

20. *ST* 1a, q. 79, a. 8, resp.

21. *ST* 1a2ae, q. 98, a. 6, resp.

22. *ST* 1a2ae, q. 98, a. 6, resp.

23. Indeed, the word *historia* is used by Aquinas to indicate the literal sense of Scripture. He makes repeated references in the *Summa* to the "historical" truth of the scriptural narrative. Thus this story is not just one with superior explanatory power for him; it is true. See, for example, *ST* 1a, q. 102, a. 1, resp

24. See, for example, Alasdair MacIntyre, *Whose Justice?* 181.

25. MacIntyre, *Whose Justice?* 177–81.

26. MacIntyre says that ultimately the structure of the *Summa* is "Pauline and Augustinian" in its emphasis on sin and the need for grace (*Whose Justice?* 181).

27. I should note a certain non-Thomistic influence in my fleshing out of practical reasoning here. I am indebted to Rosenthal's *Good Look at Evil*, in her narrative model of practical reasoning. While ultimately very different from Thomas's, her account is profoundly helpful in showing the revisability of judgment and project that is necessary for successful practical reasoning.

28. *ST* 1a2ae, q. 94, a. 6, resp.

29. See MacIntyre, *After Virtue*, 204. My discussion of MacIntyre is drawn from ch. 14 and 15 of *After Virtue*.

30. I argue at slightly greater length for the application of the notion of quest to the process of discovery of the natural law in "Towards a Narrative Understanding," 53–73.

31. As an example of legalism, I have in mind the sort of multiplication of rules within natural law ethics which has characterized recent moral theology within official Roman Catholic teaching. As an

example of the aridly theoretical, one might offer Finnis and Grisez's ethics.

32. MacIntyre, *After Virtue*, 183. See Hittinger's remarks on this rejection in *Critique*, 192–94. It may well be that MacIntyre has since moved away from his rejection of such teleology, see his *Three Rival Versions of Moral Enquiry: Encyclopedia, Genealogy, and Tradition* (Notre Dame, Ind.: University of Notre Dame Press, 1990), 127–48.

33. Nussbaum, "Crystals," 33.

34. As MacIntyre notes (*Whose Justice?* 187), Nussbaum also denies truth-values to utterances made by agents caught in tragic dilemmas insofar as she rejects "the assimilation of practical conflict to disagreement and of practical claims to beliefs" (*Fragility*, 36). Whatever conflict such a character as Agamemnon is caught within, it is not for her the conflict of contradictory moral demands; contradiction could only arise where truth-values are given to assertions. Nussbaum thus rejects one possible escape route that would permit such agents simply to falsify one of the conflicting demands and thereby resolve the dilemma: "The case [of Agamemnon] has shown us that two life-guiding commitments may conflict in a particular contingency; it certainly has not shown us that there is any logical contradiction between them, or, more to the point, that they offer bad guidance in the vast majority of deliberative situations" (*Fragility*, 47).

Nussbaum further denies that this contingent conflict arises out of a clash of beliefs; this is her intent when she refuses to assign truth-values to agents' statements by rejecting "the assimilation . . . of practical claims to beliefs." Beyond this explicit rejection, it is evident from other parts of Nussbaum's treatment of tragedy that she wishes to invest the "practical claims" that create occasions of tragic conflict with more objectivity and authority than they would possess if they were solely products of an agent's beliefs or attitudes. After all, beliefs can be mistaken beliefs, and attitudes can be misinformed attitudes. Yet it is one of her objections to those agents who seek a way out of the anxiety, the grief, even the very irresolvability of the conflict, that they are in an important way avoiding the truth about the world. This criticism is at the heart of Nussbaum's analysis of *The Golden Bowl*'s naive Maggie Verver, and it informs her treatment of Agamemnon's failings as well. But now there arises a problem. If tragic conflict is, on Nussbaum's view, neither the contradiction of moral demands nor the clash of beliefs or attitudes, what then is it? She has simply failed to characterize adequately the nature of such dilemmas.

35. Nussbaum, "Crystals," 33.

36. Ibid., 33.

37. See Nussbaum, "Discernment," 154, 170–78; see also *Fragility*, 294–305.

38. Nussbaum, "Crystals," 33.

39. *ST* 2a2ae, q. 62, a. 2.

40. *ST* 2a2ae, q. 62, a. 2 ad 2.

41. Examples of culpable perplexity are *ST* 1a2ae, q. 19, a. 6, and *ST* 3a, q. 64, a. 6. The first passage addresses whether a mistaken conscience binds; the second asks whether the wicked sin in administering the sacraments. In both, Aquinas rejects the conflicts as perplexity *simpliciter.*

42. See Nussbaum, *Fragility*, 36, and note 34, above. See also MacIntyre, *Whose Justice?* 187, for a similar observation.

43. See also Aquinas's remark at *ST* 3a, q. 64, a. 6, obj. 3: if truly caught in dilemma, a person "would be compelled to despair, as though unable to avoid sin "

44. Regarding the attempt to resolve conflicts in this way, Nussbaum says: "this is not how it *feels* to be in that situation. It does not feel like solving a puzzle, where all that is needed is to find the right answer" (*Fragility*, 32).

45. See Nussbaum's remarks ("Crystals," 34) on the kind of guilt we must encounter, on her view, in the "tangled world" of conflicting and incompatible moral claims. She calls this a "secular analogue to original sin," given that it is inescapable and "attaches to us as a structural feature of our situation in nature and in the family " But in possession of original sin, what is in fact implied is an active defection, within each person's will, away from the good; while the tendency may be "inherited," the agent becomes complicit by his or her personal choices. Nussbaum's model, on the other hand, describes a guilt which is the result not of personal choices but of the nature of the world. Maggie Verver's difficulty, in *The Golden Bowl*, is wanting, but not being able, to have a "perfect life." Would this were all original sin is.

46. Thomas Nagel and Bernard Williams have both addressed this issue. See, for example, Williams's essay "Moral Luck," in *Moral Luck:*

Philosophical Papers 1973–1980 (Cambridge: Cambridge University Press, 1981), 20–39.

47. *ST* 2a2ae, q. 124, a. 5, resp.
48. *ST* 2a2ae, q. 124, a. 3, resp.
49. *ST* 2a2ae, q. 124, a. 3, resp.

BIBLIOGRAPHY

Ackrill, J. L. "Aristotle on *Eudaimonia*." In *Essays on Aristotle's Ethics.* Ed. Amélie Oksenberg Rorty. Berkeley: University of California Press, 1980.

Aristotle. *Nicomachean Ethics.* Greek text with English translation by H. Rackham. Cambridge: Harvard University Press, 1975.

Armstrong, R. A. *Primary and Secondary Precepts in Thomistic Natural Law Teaching.* The Hague: Martinus Nijhoff, 1966.

Bourke, Vernon J. "Is Thomas Aquinas a Natural Law Ethicist?" *Monist* 58 (January 1974), 52–66.

Brown, Oscar J. *Natural Rectitude and Divine Law in Aquinas.* Toronto: Pontifical Institute of Mediaeval Studies, 1981.

Burrell, David B. *Aquinas: God and Action.* Notre Dame, Ind.: University of Notre Dame Press, 1979.

Canary, Robert, and Henry Kozicki, ed. *The Writing of History. Literary Form and Historical Understanding.* Madison: University of Wisconsin Press, 1978.

Carr, David. "Narrative and the Real World." *History and Theory* 25 (May 1986): 117–31.

———. *Time, Narrative, and History.* Bloomington: Indiana University Press, 1986.

Crites, Stephen. "The Narrative Quality of Experience." *Journal of the American Academy of Religion* 39, no. 3 (September 1971): 291–311.

Crowe, M. B. *The Changing Profile of the Natural Law.* The Hague: Martinus Nijhoff, 1977.

Donagan, Alan. *Human Ends and Human Actions: An Exploration in Thomas's Treatment.* Aquinas Lecture, 1985. Milwaukee: Marquette University Press, 1985.

Finnis, John. *Moral Absolutes: Tradition, Revision, and Truth.* Washington, D.C.: Catholic University of America Press, 1991.

―――. *Natural Law and Natural Rights*. Oxford: Clarendon Press, 1980.

Finnis, John, Germain Grisez, and Joseph Boyle. "Practical Principles, Moral Truth, and Ultimate Ends." *American Journal of Jurisprudence* (1987): 99–151.

Fortin, Ernest L. "Augustine, Thomas Aquinas, and the Problem of Natural Law." *Mediaevalia* 4 (1978): 179–208.

George, Robert P., ed. *Natural Law Theory: Contemporary Essays* Oxford: Oxford University Press, 1992.

Gilson, Etienne. *The Christian Philosophy of Saint Thomas Aquinas*. Trans. L. K. Shook, C.S.B. Reprint of 1956 ed., New York: Octagon Books, 1983.

Goerner, E. A. "On Thomistic Natural Law: The Bad Man's View of Thomistic Natural Right." *Political Theory* 7 (February 1979): 101–22.

―――. "Thomistic Natural Right: The Good Man's View of Thomistic Natural Law." *Political Theory* 11 (August 1983): 393–418.

Grisez, Germain. *Christian Moral Principles*. Vol. 1 of *The Way of the Lord Jesus*. San Francisco: Franciscan Herald Press, 1983.

―――. "The First Principle of Practical Reason." In *Aquinas: A Collection of Critical Essays*. Ed. Anthony Kenny. Garden City, N.Y.: Doubleday, 1969. Reprint, Notre Dame, Ind.: University of Notre Dame Press, 1976.

Hall, Pamela M. "Goerner on Thomistic Natural Law." *Political Theory* 18, no. 4 (November 1990): 638–49.

―――. "The Mysteriousness of the Good: Iris Murdoch and Virtue Ethics." *American Catholic Philosophical Quarterly* 64 (Summer 1990): 313–29.

―――. "Toward a Narrative Understanding of Thomistic Natural Law." *Medieval Philosophy and Theology* 2 (1992): 53–73.

Hardy, Barbara. "The Nature of Narrative." In *The Collected Essays of Barbara Hardy*, vol. 1. Sussex: Harvester Press, 1989.

Hauerwas, Stanley. *Character and the Christian Life: A Study in Theological Ethics*. San Antonio: Trinity University Press, 1975.

―――. *Truthfulness and Tragedy: Further Investigations into Christian Ethics*. Notre Dame, Ind.: University of Notre Dame Press, 1977.

Hibbs, Thomas S. "Divine Irony and the Natural Law: Speculation and Edification in Aquinas." *International Philosophical Quarterly* 30, no. 4 (December 1990): 419–29.

Hittinger, F. Russell. "After MacIntyre: Natural Law Theory, Virtue Ethics, and *Eudaimonia*." *International Philosophical Quarterly* 29 (December 1989): 449–61.

———. "Aquinas' Doctrine of Natural Law: An Account of Morality?" Paper presented at meetings of the American Catholic Philosophical Association, Boston, 1991.

———. *A Critique of the New Natural Law Theory.* Notre Dame, Ind.: University of Notre Dame Press, 1987.

———. "When It Is More Excellent to Love than to Know: The Other Side of Thomistic 'Realism'." *Proceedings of the American Catholic Philosophical Association* 57 (1983): 171–79.

Irwin, T. H. "Reason and Responsibility in Aristotle." In *Essays on Aristotle's Ethics.* Ed. Amélie Oksenberg Rorty. Berkeley: University of California Press, 1980.

Jaffa, Harry V. *Thomism and Aristotelianism* Chicago: University of Chicago Press, 1952

Jordan, Mark D. *Ordering Wisdom: The Hierarchy of Philosophical Discourse in Aquinas.* Notre Dame, Ind.: University of Notre Dame Press, 1986.

McCabe, Herbert. *What Is Ethics All About?* Washington, D.C.: Corpus Books, 1969.

McInerny, Ralph. *Aquinas on Human Action: A Theory of Practice.* Washington, D.C.: Catholic University of America Press, 1992.

———. *Ethica Thomistica.* Washington, D.C.: Catholic University of America Press, 1982.

MacIntyre, Alasdair. *After Virtue.* Notre Dame, Ind.: University of Notre Dame Press, 1981.

———. *Whose Justice? Which Rationality?* Notre Dame, Ind.: University of Notre Dame Press, 1988.

Mackey, Louis. "Entreatments of God: Reflections on Aquinas' Five Ways." *Franciscan Studies* 37 (1977): 103–19.

Mann, William E. "Jephthah's Plight: Moral Dilemma and Theism." Unpublished paper.

Murdoch, Iris. *The Sovereignty of Good.* London: Routledge and Kegan Paul, 1970.

Nelson, Daniel Mark. *The Priority of Prudence: Virtue and Natural Law in Thomas Aquinas and the Implications for Modern Ethics.* University Park, Pa: Pennsylvania State University Press, 1992.

Nussbaum, Martha Craven. "The Discernment of Perception: An Aristotelian Conception of Private and Public Rationality."

Proceedings of the Boston Area Colloquium in Ancient Philosophy.
Ed. John Cleary. New York: University Press of America, 1985.

———. "Flawed Crystals: James's *The Golden Bowl* and Literature
as Moral Philosophy." *New Literary History* 15 (Autumn 1983):
25–50.

———. *The Fragility of Goodness: Luck and Ethics in Greek Tragedy
and Philosophy.* Cambridge: Cambridge University Press, 1986.

———. "Practical Syllogisms and Practical Science." In *Aristotle's
"De Motu Animalium."* Trans. with commentary and interpretive
essays. Princeton: Princeton University Press, 1978.

O'Connor, D. J. *Aquinas and the Moral Law.* London: Macmillan,
1967.

Porter, Jean. "*De Ordine Caritatis*: Charity, Friendship, and Justice
in Thomas Aquinas' *Summa theologiae.*" *Thomist* 53 (April 1989):
197–213.

———. "Desire for God: Ground of the Moral Life in Aquinas."
Theological Studies 47 (1986). 48–68.

———. *The Recovery of Virtue: The Relevance of Aquinas for Christian
Ethics.* Louisville: Westminster/John Knox Press, 1990.

Ricoeur, Paul. *Time and Narrative.* 3 vols. Trans. Kathleen Blamey
and David Pellauer. Chicago: University of Chicago Press, 1990.

Rorty, Amélie Oksenberg "The Place of Contemplation in Aristotle's
Nicomachean Ethics." In *Essays on Aristotle's Ethics.* Ed. Amélie
Oksenberg Rorty. Berkeley: University of California Press, 1980.

Rosenthal, Abigail L. *A Good Look at Evil.* Philadelphia: Temple
University Press, 1987.

Sherman, Nancy. *The Fabric of Character: Aristotle's Theory of Virtue.*
Oxford: Clarendon Press, 1989.

Staley, Kevin M. "Happiness: The Natural End of Man?" *Thomist* 53,
no. 2 (April 1989): 215–34.

Strauss, Leo. *Natural Right and History.* Chicago: University of Chicago Press, 1950.

Thomas Aquinas. *Summa theologiae.* Latin text. 5 vols. Ottawa: Institute of Medieval Studies, 1941.

———. *Summa theologica.* Trans. Fathers of the English Dominican
Province. New York: Benziger Brothers, 1947. Reprint, Westminster, Md.: Christian Classics, 1981.

Wiggins, David. "Deliberation and Practical Reason." In *Essays on
Aristotle's Ethics.* Ed. Amélie Oksenberg Rorty. Berkeley: University of California Press, 1980.

INDEX

ABOUT THE AUTHOR

Pamela M. Hall received her Ph.D. from Vanderbilt University and is currently Associate Professor of Philosophy and Women's Studies at Emory University. In addition to *Narrative and the Natural Law*, she has published a number of articles in scholarly journals.